THAT WAS /
THAT WAS

The Story of a Radio Programme
1979–2017

Libby Purves

That Was Midweek That Was
The Story of a Radio Programme 1980–2017
by Libby Purves

© Libby Purves 2017

Published in 2017
by Songsend Books

A catalogue card for this book is available from the British Library.

ISBN: 978-0-9557085-1-0

Cover Designs © Roger Hardy

Typesetting by TJ INK (www.tjink.co.uk)

Printed and bound by TJ International, Cornwall, UK

"Keeping people amused is an inexact science."
Terry Wogan

To everyone who worked on it, and every guest who ever turned up. Especially after a late night.

INTRODUCTION

Why write a biography and obituary of the Radio 4 Midweek programme? There are plenty of books about the BBC, and a few about Radio 4, ranging from the scholarly to the chatty. In most of these such a programme will rarely merit more than a footnote. It has pretended to be nothing but a loose chain of not particularly newsworthy interviews and light conversations, a nine o'clock relief after the rat-a-tat news and conflict of the Today programme.

In my own life, it was more than a footnote, though not the largest part: a couple of days' work each week, culminating in fifty-seven – or latterly forty-three – minutes live on air. But when, like a red-nosed old variety artist, the show finally got hooked offstage by a Radio 4 Controller (the seventh CR4 since it started, under the ninth Director-General) I started to think about it. And I found myself suddenly aware that I had done it for up to forty-five weeks each year, for thirty-three years. Years which span, with pleasing neatness, a bit over half my time on this planet.

I have hosted Midweeks through the birth of one child and the death two decades later of another, the loss of both parents and a brother. Those years have seen four months operating with a paralyzed arm and three bouts of eye surgery, which for a time required me, to general amusement, to print my notes in a 24-point font. I have found solace in work by continuing through two bouts of clinical depression, four house moves and ten years assisting incompetently with my husband's horse-drawn organic farm, frequently breaking off from wrestling with the research notes to chase sheep.

Friendships were born over those years (one or two from meetings on the programme). Assorted parallel jobs have risen and fallen: novelist, columnist, Times theatre critic, editorial consultant to an insurance company magazine, undercover editor of the Ritz Hotel customer mag. But always Midweek returned each autumn as the swallows flew south. There must have been around six thousand guests. Though some, admittedly, turned up more than once.

So, I thought OK: give the old show a biography in case nobody else does. The final spur for the idea came three weeks before the axe fell, when the celebrity milliner Stephen Jones came on the programme. On that day in autumn 2016 he proudly informed me that he'd been on before, "though you might not remember it". It was in 1983, when he was launching his graduation collection. Stephen remembered that his fellow guests included Sir Harold Wilson and Max Wall: one a retired Prime Minister, the other staging a comedy comeback at 75, with a career dating back to panto in 1922. The comedian Tim Brooke-Taylor was on, too. Indeed, a typical Midweek can be like a particularly random game of Consequences.

The Wilson & Wall reminder also made me feel a bit like the fossilized dinosaur brain recently discovered in Bexhill. Or, to put it more kindly, like a scrap of history, deserving at least the corner of a dusty glass case in the Museum of Lost Radio. I can at least say that I did this show for ten years longer than Hilda Ogden was on Coronation Street.

I thought further, and reflected sadly that I would actually be happier if the Controller had kept the programme and just ditched me for a new presenter. This moment of personal obsolescence, after all, is something all sane presenters half-expect at every contract time. One day, you know perfectly well, the management will look at you with the kind of amazed horror that one feels on opening a forgotten kitchen drawer, bin-bag in hand. And that'll be it. As the great Robert Robinson said, refusing to sob and rant when they axed Stop the Week fifteen years earlier, "I am only the hired help."

But I didn't feel that Midweek itself deserved the heave-ho. It had grown over the years – organically, largely accidentally – into something different and rather fascinating: a casual meeting place for people of utterly different experiences and qualities, who surprisingly often bond and find shared human ground.

This is where Thora Hird met Bruce Dickinson of Iron Maiden; where Denis Healey, ex-Chancellor, was introduced to the principal of the London School of Striptease; where plodding old Ken from Coronation Street, Bill Roache, struck up a friendship with the Cuban ballet star Carlos Acosta (Acosta was fascinated and admiring of his army stories and Druid beliefs). Here Frank Zappa and Paddy Moloney of the Chieftains met and stayed friends; here Damon Albarn first met the artist Suzi Winstanley, his long-term partner. Here Marmaduke Hussey, the improbable toff Chairman of the BBC in the '80s and '90s, came on for a chat after he left that post and during a random conversation involving cannabis, merrily said that he wished he'd ever "tried some of that stuff".

People faff about devising exciting new "formats" for broadcast shows, but this one had a perfectly simple chemistry. Because it was live, everyone round that table knew they were in the same boat, vibrating the same frequency for all to hear. Because it was live, famous people also knew that unlike in a recorded or print interview, they could not be cut about and selectively quoted. There's an honesty in going live because the presenter can be flatly contradicted if she raises something untrue from past press reports.

Thirdly, because such a show is not in a wire-strangled overlit TV studio but in a small hutch with sound-absorbing walls, nobody is self-conscious about the way they look. They can – if shy – effectively disappear simply by going silent. That is a surprisingly relaxing aspect of radio work. When webcams were put into some Radio 4 studios, veteran presenters (outside of news) tended to rebel. The legend has it that Jenni Murray defiantly draped her pashmina over hers. I did once twist an early one to face the wall, but apparently, it was never live anyway. "If you want people to goggle at us like TV puppets," we radio stalwarts felt, "give us TV fees and a make-up room!"

Because the guests were so mixed – often by accident because someone suddenly became available and someone else dropped out on Tuesday – there was also on Midweek a curious and benign effect, in which oft-interviewed celebrities or people of power expressed a different side of themselves. This is not because of any skill of mine but because they were sitting next to an astrophysicist, a woman who raised a score of foster-children, someone who walked across Antarctica or survived kidnap and war. Sometimes it was simply someone doing a useful and unsung job: community midwifery, a census of estuary seals, road planning. In these circumstances, it is impossible for anyone to behave like a precious diva, or to put on their accustomed armour and crank out all the well-worn quips. We never, for instance, interviewed any comedian or artiste "in character": not even Dame Edna. It would have been awkward for the other people at the table who were required to be themselves. One cabaret singer of the Weimar-wannabe generation, who answers only to her professional name, never joined us for just that reason.

Celebrity interviews in particular benefit from that mixed frank humanity. However raked-over by accustomed fame you are, you're going to be enlivened to new responses when you're in conversation with a young unknown artist who makes casts of roadkill, or a chap who carves pictures on grains of rice through a microscope and explains that he has to take beta-blockers to slow his heartbeat while he does it.

So, I have enjoyed this curious programme, and it has survived many a sneer from that glum cadre of commentators who lament "lack of substance" (a swipe from colleague Simon Elmes himself, in his normally emollient book "And Now on Radio 4"). Some radio critics hate it, possibly with a smidgeon of envy because it sounds fun. Some general commentators – God bless the Guardian, the people's friend! – drop disdainful references to "middlebrow tosh". But to hell with all that: we held up with our two-million-plus listeners, sometimes beating the more chin-strokingly respectable In Our Time and Start the Week. We gave live airtime not only to public achievers but far more often to people who would otherwise only be heard in a carefully pre-edited segment, or in safe curated likeable soundbites on "The Listening Project". It has been fun. I've sometimes groaned at a particularly dense, difficult set of books and research notes (it's like doing an A level in a hurry some weeks, when it's Ethiopian history or Astrophysics). But I've liked it. The producers – over a dozen through the years – have overwhelmingly been creative, clever, inventive, good to work with and even more fun to argue with.

But it is over now. So there's an instinct to share the most vivid and memorable parts of the experience, assisted by random dredging of the memories of former team members. So here we are: how it was and how it was done. As far as we all can, in the dark backward and abysm of time, remember.

THE BEGINNINGS: SEVENTIES AND EIGHTIES

Midweek was born sometime in the late 1970s: indeed, on the day its demise was announced, the BBC press office seemed unable to work out exactly when, so plumped for 1979 and gave Russell Harty as its original presenter. Actually, memory recalls that before Russell's eccentric charm rescued it, Midweek had a rocky start in the '70s. Start the Week with Richard Baker had been established in the early '70s, as a general talk show rather than today's more intellectual feast. A series of phone-in shows had ended, and Radio 4 around that time decided to experiment with Rollercoaster, in which the same presenter – Baker – meandered on from 9 to 11 a.m. with a mixed magazine. It was born of the worry that programme junctions cause people to switch off. Indeed, they often do: Radio 4 listeners tend to be determined and focused people who haughtily resent being what TV executives call "an inherited audience", as if they were chattels or slaves to be passed on. But Rollercoaster was pretty awful. David Hatch is quoted endearingly in Elmes' book as saying that he had wanted to "shake the trees a bit", but probably shouldn't have had a presenter who actually "was the tree". Richard Baker went peaceably back to Start the Week's old format until he left in 1987.

Meanwhile Midweek emerged with Desmond Wilcox as chairman, he having been lately edged out of his TV executive post. I also seem to recall a bizarre period when Sylvia Syms hosted it, with an overcrowded panoply of spare interviewers. But as I say, even the press office doesn't seem sure before '79, and it may be a bad dream. But I clearly remember my husband Paul dismissing the idea of my being involved, even as a "guest interviewer" sidekick, when I was asked to work alongside Russell Harty in 1981 (they titled it "Russell Harty's People", desperate for celebrity stardust). The show's reputation was by that time so poor that it was not unreasonable for Paul to say, "I wouldn't bother. Midweek never did anyone any favours. Be careful."

Russell Harty rescued Midweek. Working alongside him as guest interviewer was a treat. I had things to learn about conducting general Radio 4 talk, because I came from local radio followed by hard news (I was a Today presenter for three-and-a-half years to 1981). Sitting near Russell as he rambled obliquely through the guest list was marvellously educative and refreshing. It taught me about the value of the apparently vague question, and the need to deviate from the notes and research when an interesting trail opened up. On one occasion Russell got so engrossed with the mountaineer Chris Bonington that he completely forgot the clock and the fourth guest, and ended the programme with a cry of "Oh dear, I've run out of time … will you come back next week?" The subject meekly did so.

Another time he neatly filleted the purity campaigner Mary Whitehouse, who tended to go on a bit about how she represented the Decent Moral Ordinary Housewife's Point Of View. Russell, with that childlike inquisitiveness which could never offend but always hit the mark, suddenly asked apropos nothing, "Do you do a lot of cooking, Mary?". Her startled reply made it instantly crystal clear that she had not been any kind of "ordinary housewife" for many years, but a tough, full-time, seasoned one-note lobbyist.

But my favourite Russell memory is of when we did the show live from Paris – no idea why. We had Charlotte Rampling and her then husband Jean-Michel Jarre on. During his normal dreamy note-gazing stage before they all arrived, I asked Russell, "Do they count as one guest or two?"

"Ooh, good idea. I'll just ask them outright, How many of you are there?"

From that day onward it was a programme-planning catchphrase: the question one never actually asks but which Russell immediately declared was the most profound information you could ever ask of anyone: "How many of you are there?" We often discussed this in connection with whoever was the "birthday guest" I had to interview. I nearly asked David Frost once, suspecting that nobody could be as smooth as he seemed on air, "David, seriously, how many of you are there?"

Russell left the programme and Henry Kelly took over chairmanship, still with me as guest interviewer (this was during a curious period when I both had my first baby and accidentally edited Tatler for six months). But in 1983 I succeeded to the chair, with producer Pete Estall championing me. The Controller of Radio 4, Monica Sims, was against the idea and had seemingly blocked it earlier, to the point that in frustration I managed to get a direct interview in her office to ask her why. She had, by the way, earlier disliked my Today presenter role, and I was told that her reluctance was overruled by Aubrey Singer, Managing Director Radio and a great champion of women on the air. It was he who sent me to do the Today programme live from China in 1978, a heady time when the Democracy Wall Movement meant the regime acquiesced briefly in the expression of discontent, and accepted some opening-up to the West. The live show was a mildly historic event which excited the Chinese broadcasters no end, as they even had to record the News.

Anyway, at first Monica Sims denied having anything to do with vetoing me on Midweek, then said something along the lines of, "Well, I prefer you doing documentaries". I explained that Radio 4 documentaries, which I would still make, were such lovingly crafted things that they paid less per hour than babysitting or cleaning windows. I never forgot her response:

"Oh, is money an issue then? But you're married ..."

So much for 1970s women in management. But to be fair, Monica Sims was, on the whole, an excellent Controller and two years later produced the very important "Women in BBC Management" report, stirring up the blokery and laying, among other things, the foundations for flexible work and jobshares. So maybe it was just me she didn't like. Fair enough.

Anyway, she gave in and it began. Russell, generous as ever, actually listened live to the first show I hosted and rang the studio afterwards to say well done. A lovely man he was. The programme was still fifty-five minutes long, and still had a guest interviewer for the Birthday Guest: a gimmick devised to prevent the whole programme being taken up by people with something to plug. Stepping aside for the ten-minute space of that birthday interview was interesting for the main presenter. You could listen without having to speak, pick up points and interject. Very occasionally one might have to rescue an interviewer sliding into a pit, but more often just to amplify.

Among those guest interviewers, memory recalls several unexpected names. Derek Jamieson was one. He was recruited as a tough tabloid veteran – he had edited the Express, Star, and News of the World and been lampooned by Private Eye under the name of Sid Yobbo. But he promptly dismayed us and torpedoed a hard-won interview with Robert Maxwell by playing it unaccountably soft (I think a looming job in a Maxwell company may have been involved). Actually, Maxwell was hell anyway: one of those personalities so large and threatening that they seem to use up all the oxygen in the room. Meeting him, I understood more than ever before or since how tyrannies flourish and overbearing personalities crush quieter ones. But I wish we had been tougher.

A splendid guest interviewer was Bernard Levin, who came on to interview his old mate Sir Robin Day. When I taxed Day, lightly, with an unnecessarily aggressive interviewing style, he harrumphed "Don't know what you mean!" – and may even have added "Young lady", as chaps often did back then. Levin, sharp as a razor and wholly unfazed by the great bruiser's Maxwellian ability to use up all the oxygen, nipped in and defended me. "You know perfectly well what she means Robin. You do it all the time."

Other birthday interviewers were diverse: one was a young chap from the Guardian called James Naughtie, doing his first live broadcasts. And I remember Christina Hardyment, the writer and scholar of children's literature, crossing swords quite sharply with Richard Adams, the author of Watership Down. Edna Healey at one stage filled the role, though I cannot trace who she interviewed; Jill Freud talked with Diana Quick. Others were rising broadcasters, including for a while the late John Diamond.

One long-term holder of the job was the young Ian Hislop of Private Eye: sharp and interesting, but at first bravely new to live radio. I remember (he does too) his interview with

Spike Milligan. Ian wrote his notes in what turned out to be water-soluble felt-tip. In those days, incredible now, there was a bottle of champagne opened for the Birthday Guest: a silly business, like all eating-and-drinking on the radio, but typical of the period. Ian tipped a glass over onto his notes, which he had written in champagne-soluble green felt-tip pen. His questions and prompts melted rapidly into watercolour soup before our eyes. And before Spike's: the great man gave an evil grin, but proceeded with great courtesy to co-operate more than previously and complete a good and revealing interview. Well, a string of jokes, but that in itself is revealing.

On another occasion, Ian was confronted with Jeffrey Archer, who suddenly and with real aggression accused him of being a leftie, and announced with pride that he had – Ian remembers with amazement – "paid four hundred and forty thousand pounds in tax" that year. Ian coped fine, and it was clear enough to me that Jeffrey was messing around for effect. But when the Archer-bomb detonated I remember our producer, Victor Lewis-Smith, nominally a warrior on the side of comic chaos, unexpectedly squeaking down the talkback. "Make it all friendly again!"

Maybe there was some executive looming behind him, I couldn't see. Occasionally management do turn up behind the glass, like exotic tropical fish, but they sometimes have the tact to stay out of the presenter's eyeline. Actually, one live presenter to this day is so lairy of being looked at through glass that he insists on a special bit of cardboard being put up to screen his privacy.

But of all the Midweek producers down the decades, Vic Lewis-Smith was the wildest card. His metier has always been comedy, the angriest and most savagely obscene he can get away with, so he was an unusual appointment for Radio 4. His ideas were sometimes brilliantly interesting – especially when his eclectic musical knowledge was involved – and his taste in guests was entertaining. He once tried to book a chap whose cabaret act was melting a block of ice with a blowtorch, and did get another whose act was making musical slurping noises with a washing-up bowl on his pot belly. Unfortunately, Vic hated me, or at least everything he thought I stood for: he saw me as a mumsy, home-this-afternoon, Woman's-Houry creature and suspected that we had been put in harness because I would emit old-R4 "sensibleness" and moderate his louche creativity. It worked to some extent, but at my expense. I had to be far more careful on the air than I would naturally be, owing to the distraction of Vic's persistent shouting down the talkback. When he left and the earphones went blissfully quiet, I found myself liberated to ask riskier questions and make jokes. The ones he might have liked. Ironic.

On the announcement of Midweek's ending in late 2016, Vic emerged from the distant past deploying Twitter with characteristic grace:

"So Midweek is axed. This was my attempt to destroy it as its producer years ago. Libby Purves still makes me puke."

He added some rant about my being the "self-styled voice of Middle England", which is not a styling I would ever claim. He also tweeted, "She threw a fucking chair at me cos I refused to let her kids' choir sing Silent Night on the show. H. Jacques/ Stalin in a frock."

Ah, the post-truth age! My only child at the time was barely two years old, hardly a chorister; I would never make such a dreary suggestion anyway, and a presenter's power is nil. Mind you, I did threaten to throw a chair at him, may even have picked it up. But that would be out of mere frustration when the research packs got worse and worse. One week, a fourth guest in the envelope he sent was represented only by a brief newspaper clipping, the story format unfortunately symmetrical both sides, so with no indication as to which side of the clipping I was supposed to plan an interview around. And while we're correcting history, I didn't "ban" his attempt to book a dwarf-throwing act. I just said that the dwarf involved should be keen, fully consenting, and join in the interview. It was the head of department, Alan Rogers, who took fright at that booking.

One could sense that managerial fright rising week after week, but Vic had a good run: it was a period when "Alternative Comedy" was thought to be the only way to communicate with Youth, and it is to Radio 4's honour that its senior managers tremblingly but determinedly sought out the louche 'n youthful. As for me, I had a young child at home and plenty else to think about, so I had no difficulty shrugging off the concerns of work at the end of a shift. If, getting in on a Tuesday, I found that one guest was promising to bang a nail up his nose live on the air and that another "promised to keep it clean but might need controlling", that could be dealt with when it happened. Real life in Suffolk was more important.

Vic did two stellar things, though. He booked the eccentric Stanley Owen Green, who used to walk up and down Oxford Street with a placard saying LESS LUST BY LESS PROTEIN: MEAT FISH BIRD EGG CHEESE PEAS BEAN LENTILS AND SITTING. I was delighted, and remain proud that although Green patrolled a stone's throw from Broadcasting House for twenty-five years, we were the only programme ever to invite him in. As a guest, he was fine: not mad, quite lucid as he related his views, his naval background and the physicalities of being a human billboard. The present-day Vic now claims on Twitter, "He believed in less sitting but his s's came out as sh's which was my sole reason for booking him: to irritate Purves." It didn't.

Nor was I less than delighted by the joke, one of the finest ever to dismay a Radio 4 Controller, of Vic's booking the lugubrious "Oh Yus" cockney actor-comedian, Arthur Mullard to replace me when I was off one week. This was well before Mullard's history of domestic violence and abuse was known. It was a totally scripted, pre-recorded programme, a spoof Midweek complete with audible talkback interjections. In our normal live shows these interruptions, heard only by me, were a Vic speciality: on one occasion, he kept shouting "Scapegoat! Scapegoat!" during an interview, and when I asked later what the hell that was about, he said something like, "He has been made a scapegoat for the failure of contemporary music to engage with …" whatever.

"But Vic, we never discussed that. Nor was it in the notes …"

"I only just thought of it!"

Anyway, the Mullard programme was funny and I kept a tape for years until I lost it in a house move. Victor's Twitterrage gets it wrong again – "Purves hated the programme, the awful humourless cow. She could kill off comedy at 100 paces and still can. Good riddance."

It is odd, reading that, to remember the day Vic left the show: I gave him a leaving present to sum up his temperament and our relationship. It was one of those baseball hats with an arm coming out of it brandishing a hammer to hit the wearer on the head. He laughed, and I deludedly thought we parted friends. Sort of.

What he may remember with more accuracy is the earlier intervention in our working relationship by poor Alan Rogers, head of what was then known as CAMP – Current Affairs Magazine Programmes. Alan called us both in for a sort of marriage-guidance counselling session, made us shake hands and respectively say "I respect you as a producer" and "I respect you as a presenter". We both thought that was so funny that we actually bonded quite nicely afterwards, giggling down the curving corridors of Broadcasting House from Alan's office to ours.

But before long Alan moved him to Start the Week, and moved Ian Strachan from that programme to produce Midweek. Unfortunately, Alan was a lay preacher and full of a shining Christian honesty which compelled him to inform Richard Baker of Start the Week that the move was because "Libby found Vic difficult to work with". Managers note: such openness may be virtuous but it is really not a tactful way to signal any working relationship. Luckily, Richard Baker was an old-stager and didn't object. Before long, though, Vic created waves on Start the Week: one programme I remember had Ruby Wax being marginally obscene in the presence of a child, which made intensely uncomfortable listening. There was also a bizarre booking of the Roland Rat puppet from TV-am alongside the dignified septuagenarian composer Gian Carlo Menotti. Who didn't seem to get the joke. Vic's comedy career went on elsewhere, not without highspots.

That these things could happen says much about the old loose, collegiate structure of BBC Radio: producers were trusted, guests not filtered through a central booking team, and the concept of "compliance" was not yet coined, still less the bizarre turning of it into a transitive verb, as in "Has Emma complied that recording yet?" The overall editor of the talk programmes was an old-school post-war Hungarian émigré called Michael Ember, with immaculately polished shoes, who would merely raise his eyebrows when we tumbled back upstairs to the office after a show. We rarely got a comment beyond "We-elll … Zat didn't entirely bring the Corporation into disrepute". He had studied psychology and criminology, and later invented Antony Clare's programme, In the Psychiatrist's Chair. That this fastidious intellectual was in charge of Vic, his louche guests and chair-brandishing presenter is piquant to remember.

So, on we go into the later '80s. It was, by the way, during this period that the three shows punctuating the week got their nicknames. Richard Branson had been on Start the Week and as it happened, his auntie Clare Hoare, who kept rare black sheep in Norfolk, was on Midweek two days later. Branson reportedly said to her, "Yeah, I was on Pluggers, on Monday, and you were on Nutters on Wednesday." So the shows became "Pluggers", "Nutters" and (for Robert Robinson's argumentatively eloquent Stop the Week) "Wankers".

A HOUSE POET AND A PRIME MATRIARCH

Another regular, for a couple of years, was Nigel Forde, the calmly witty, erudite poet who at one point hosted the Radio 4 book show. Nigel's task, apart from general joining-in, was to write during the hour a poem summarizing the guests and conversations. Some are in his collections, "Fluffy Dice" and "The Dust Behind the Door". Vic had booked him, though he outlasted that brief regime, and he was a gem: the fact that he vanished from the network later, after serving as the most modest and learned book show presenter of any period, is sad. He would arrive with a little black notebook and listen intently from the end of the table. Sometimes he would have a few lines prepared on the season, but he rose specifically to every guest. He describes his more domestic poems as "Giles cartoons in verse" and there was something Giles-like about them: broad comedy founded on understanding of the small frustrations of life – like winter, when "the bland and biddable butter suddenly / Savages the bread".

His romanticism, always slightly sent-up, was a joy too: one poem title was "English Angels smiled with English smiles upon the scenery / Which is why the whole of England's like a garden in a Deanery". John Major and George Orwell between them couldn't improve on that, even with those old maids bicycling to Holy Communion in the early morning mist. The rest of the poem grows ever darker.

He wrote a sharp one about the green room atmosphere before the programme: "A strange sort of place to be / It has a perplexing no-man's-landish / ambiguity / Especially at 8.32 in the bowels of the BBC". And his books include a few of his responses to actual guests, from Laurie Lee to John Dankworth by way of Julie Felix. Here are a few scraps, by kind permission.

"Anthony Burgess' learning
And Klangfarbenmelodie
Can stretch from St Paul to Napoleon via
Steatopygous Enderby."

He brilliantly described Ivor Cutler:

"An architect of the absurd
A suavely surrealists songster
A dour Scots Magritte of the Word."

And of Marguerite Fawdry, owner of Pollocks' Toy Theatres, he wrote:

"Ah, Pollocks! The splendid proscenium arch
In the gold of a bygone age
Contrasting, as in real theatre, with
The rubbish on the stage."

Sometimes he combined all the guests, a tricky one, but note this cricketing elegance:

"An attacking field for Dickie Bird;
Anne Robinson, lithe, assured;
John Duffield, short square Lego;
And an extremely silly Forde."

(John Duffield was an artist who had designed for Lego Group Australia.)

He was a master of the neat pun: when Jane Glover, the conductor, was on he concluded "Karajan conducting till / Your Boults begin to Rattle", and the horn player Barry Tuckwell was "the man behind the Hinde-myth".

It was a virtuoso demonstration nearly every week. Nicholas Coleridge, then of Harpers & Queen, was teased about "Entertaining Mr Sloane". The Bishop of Durham's famous line about the Resurrection as "a conjuring trick with bones" turned up when teamed with a musician as a challenge to "reduce Don Giovanni to a conjuring trick with trombones".

One or two were near the knuckle. Professor Sir Alan Peacock had chaired the 1985 committee into the funding of the BBC, at a time when we were in the doghouse as far as the Tories were concerned: a bunch of what Denis Thatcher called pinkoes. Peacock's report in the end concluded, to some ministers' disgust, that advertising on the BBC was impracticable. He also, if I remember, sapiently predicted that government censorship would become pointless in the age of satellite and subscription TV.

Forde's poem is worth quoting in full:

"Alan Peacock's our birthday guest
Surrounded by BBC
Why is he waving that big white flat
And smiling so sheepishly?
Unfortunately the Professor's report
Has come a bit too late:
I came in this morning, and Broadcasting House
Was stamped with a huge sell-by date.
But then, listeners writing to Radio Times
If we take them seriously
Think it's always been stamped with "Best Before
Nineteen-fifty-three."

The Thatcher years were tough for cheeky broadcasters. Forde got away with a couple of ripe moments: when Roger Law (co-creator of Spitting Image) was on, Nigel wrote about "the iron mistress of the twofold face / Which being rubber, quite appropriately / Stretches – like her credibility". As for John Wells, after he had played the Prime Minister's husband in "Anyone for Denis?", the lines:

"He's shown us all this morning
If we needed to be shown
The febrile, fatuous fuddled face
Of the power behind the crone."

We got away with those, though right up to her political demise in 1990 there was intense anxiety about references to our controversial prime minister. The trouble was that because of her style and the changes she wrought, she came to seem not so much first-among-equals as Prime Matriarch. Anti-Thatcherism was simply there, inescapable, hanging in the air or blowing from unexpected quarters. It really felt for a period as if the whole nation was a rebellious sullen teenager trying to break free of an overstrict mother. Even my small son, in his first term at school in 1987, came home chanting to the tune of We Shall Not Be Moved, "Miss-us Thatcher, put her in the bin! Put the lid on, Sellotape her in!"

Because this stroppy mood inevitably crept onto the air, the BBC was, as the lady would have said, proper frit! Recent papers released by the Margaret Thatcher Foundation reveal that by 1986 and the Libya invasion, so violent were the attacks by her minister Norman Tebbit (lovingly known then as the Chingford Polecat) that the PM herself told him to back off.

Anyway, a diktat went out that in general talk shows there should be no, repeat no, disobliging references to the PM. If possible, no reference at all. "No Thatcher-bashing!" they said. And we tried, oh how we tried. But it kept happening.

Suppose you had a comedian, a collector of vintage medical instruments, an octogenarian who had passed her first A level, and the late Bishop of Leicester, Richard Rutt, aficionado and historian of knitting. We would put the fear of God into the comedian, obviously; but then foolishly presume the others were safe. But the Bishop, I remember, slid sideways from his casting-on and plain-and-purl themes to take a clerical swipe at the PM – it was shortly after Bishop David Sheppard's "Bias to the Poor" speeches. The medical-instrument man demonstrated a catheter beautifully forged with bronze bits or whatever, and said in passing that proper money was spent in those days, before today's "Thatcher NHS cuts". And the octogenarian lady – though this may have been in a different week – was asked jovially whether she had any more ambitions and promptly quavered, "I'd like to see that wicked woman go before I die."

So we would stagger out of the studio gripping our heads, and the producer of the day would go sadly upstairs to be reproved. Meanwhile, over on Radios 1 and 2 mischief was slipping into the playlists: Dylan growling "I don wanna work on Maggie's farm no more!" and Rod Stewart singing

"Maggie I jus' can' take it anymore" caused wincing on the management floors. One folk producer got pained protests over the Liverpool traditional tribute to Maggie May who "robbed so many sailors, an' the captains of the whalers …".

In all fairness, it must be said that I doubt very much Mrs Thatcher herself gave a damn about any of this stuff. Her ministers were more likely to be the trouble.

Another cause for Radio 4 irritation during that period was an outbreak of renovation in Broadcasting House. When you had a live programme, you were supposed to get a "knocking chit" to stop hammering noises intruding. The system rarely worked. Sometimes shy guests were seriously distracted by it, lost their thread of thought and needed rescue. Once – only once – I was so infuriated that I urged listeners on air to phone in and protest. I doubt any of them got through.

Anyhow, Nigel Forde was a gem during his few years with us. He did Ernie Wise, Rowan Atkinson, Kenneth Williams, Bruce Kent the anti-nuclear campaigner, Peter de Savary and John Hillaby; he found Colonel Blashford-Snell "Quieter and modester / Than the cross I expected between Columbus, Dan Dare and C.S. Forester". When Group Captain Townsend came on (nervous, speaking little of his non-marriage to Princess Margaret), Nigel wrote gentle lines. He described Mike Leigh's theatre work as "A sort of revenge Alan Ayckbourn / Without his proscenium archness". Then Ayckbourn himself was described with Forde brilliance: "While he's tickling you under the armpits, he bashes you on the shin". He did Roy Hudd and Michael Grade, and the cartoonist Gerald Scarfe who "By a kind of visual metonymy / Can criticize a nation's whole economy". Nigel Forde, in short, was the sort of figure Radio 4 needs. When his elegant tenure ended I lamented it, and still do. His books are still worth reading.

CUTTING OFF A LEG: A TROUBLESOME BOYLE

Those first memories come from the period when Midweek lasted from 09.05 to 10.00, and so benefited from a guest interviewer or a glorious gimmick like the Forde poem. For me it also provided the fun, cherished by all ex-Today presenters and live DJs, of talking up to the Greenwich Time Signal without "crashing the pips". I never did crash, not that I can remember. But there was one exciting moment when the last speaker was an aged American film producer in his nineties. He had been fascinating, but as the last minute approached and I tried to start my round of thanks, the old man began "There's one other little story I'd like to tell, and it's about your very own Queen Mother …".

I gulped. And reflected "Oh hell, this might be the old boy's last chance to tell his royal anecdote". So I would risk the network's displeasure. It's only radio, after all, not an intensive care bed. But the chap's ancient lizard eye slid sideways to the clock, and with a crafty grin he continued, telescoping and elegantly completing his story just in time to give me five seconds to sign off. What a pro. American guests nearly always are.

The days of pip-wrangling, however, were numbered. From 1992 to 2000, during the reign of the managerialist, compulsively reorganizationalist Director-General John Birt, there was not only a Thatcher-bashing terror but a wave of neurotic anxiety over ratings and audience surveys. It was a time of internal markets and of "bi-mediality": vertical management structures according to genre, so that Radio departments moved under the dark wing of TV executives who didn't necessarily understand it. It was a time of great political anxiety, and in Radio, real fear for its future. I recently rediscovered in the depths of my PC the text of an inflammatory lecture I gave to the Radio Academy in the middle of the decade. In a career-suicidal mood I said we should debate the motion: "That the BBC is no longer a fit guardian for quality speech radio". My line was that entrusting its fate to executives with a TV mindset was dangerous: I said that the Eric Gill statue on Broadcasting House of Prospero, the tall and powerful figure apparently protecting the nimble Ariel, was more like an image of television strangling the frail brave spirit that was radio. Goodness, I was cross! Here are some excerpts.

'I would much rather not be here at all. In 25 years around BBC Radio I have made it a point of pride to avoid BBC politics. I consider the prime relationship of a programme maker to be with the listener; the second relationship with the interviewees and subjects, because you have a responsibility to render them honestly; and only lastly with the management. If you're making a programme – whether it's about stair rods or toasted cheese or twentieth-century philosophers – you, the maker, should be joyfully obsessed with stair rods or toasted cheese or Bertrand Russell ... and how to convey the excitement of them. You should not be worrying about the management, or the commissioning editors, or the government either. For some years, I managed not to even know the names or jobs of any of the management. The point was the programmes; the BBC was the vehicle; management was what went on under the bonnet.'

'It is the uniqueness of the form of communication, the art form of reflective, intelligent, speech radio, which makes it important not to lose it. Nothing personal, but if pressed, I would say that Radios 1 and 2 do little which couldn't be done by a commercial service. 5 live is still a baby, and the jury's out on it. Radio 4, on the other hand, is replicated nowhere else in the world, and could not be reinvented from scratch on a self-funding basis. It has its faults – God, it can be cosy and smug, and gratuitously boring – but basically it is a marvel. Direct communication, mind to mind, democratic, portable, open.

It is the place where the best comedy is born. Because of its cheapness and speed, it can be daring; from Hancock to Alan Partridge, from the Goons to the News Quiz, it has fed television's imagination. It produces more rigorous, questioning news analysis than television; again, cheapness helps, and the emphasis on words rather than pictures.

Its documentaries are – again because of cheapness, and because of the peculiar penetrative power of radio into the brain – on the whole, more memorable and far more varied …

Sometimes people who care about radio lobby for what Melvyn Bragg dubbed an Intellectual FM, a purely high-culture station, but to me the eclectic, batty variety of Radio 4 is important. For the long-distance driver, the homeworker, craft worker, or – as I know from experience – the person in a hospital bed recovering from double eye surgery – it is a precious thing to switch on at random and end up accidentally better-informed about Icelandic sagas or the medieval church or particle physics. Radio 4, the Home Service, has been a great boon to Britain.

Why are radio resources, in real terms, so much lower than the network used to have? Why is there so little confidence in the nature of Radio 4 that its leaders have to rely on footling and hideously expensive focus-group research to tell them where to go? Why, in short, is running Radio 4 such a poisoned chalice?

If you keep shedding a lot of your craft base, your technical core – and getting rid of squads of experienced programme-makers – then in the television world this is not an irretrievable error. Other people may well pick them up. There's lots of television out there. There is hardly any type of programme BBC television makes which isn't replicated somewhere by a commercial channel – except perhaps education and some children's programmes. BBC and commercial now buy from the same TV production outfits. There is no technique that BBC television has developed which is not also needed by commercial television – therefore, craftsmen and women have somewhere else to go if the BBC won't use them. The same goes for disc jockeys; and news jockeys too, up to a point. But if the BBC doesn't run a crafted, quality, cerebral, cultured radio service, nobody will. Britain – and the BBC – cannot dare take the liberties with radio and the way it's run that it can with television. It's just not the same game. If the BBC doesn't make Casualty or Home Front or Blankety Blank– what the hell, someone else might. If the BBC doesn't make File on 4 or The Long March of Everyman or I'm sorry I Haven't a Clue or Spoonface Steinberg – nobody will. We may dream that a Getty or a Gulbenkian will suddenly pour millions into Talk Radio and take serious BBC Radio on, head to head, just for the sake of doing good to the nation ... but it's only a dream. What we have, we need. We have to cherish it.

That's really the fear that provoked me to ask in print the question whether the BBC – which, corporately, now mainly sees itself as a major player in the vast and hawkish international television industry – is actually any longer the right sort of organization to run something as thoughtful, unhawkish, adult, discursive and intellectually adventurous as Radio 4 should be. If we were inventing the whole shebang from scratch, would radio have anything to do with the television industry at all? Would you put Robert Maxwell in charge of a Cambridge college? Would you think that the Royal Shakespeare Company was safe in the hands of the Disney organization? Could a merchant bank run a good street carnival?

We have all seen what happens when giant pan-global hotel chains take over quirky, likeable small hotels, or multinationals take over small craftsmanlike boatyards, or adventurous magazines and publishers get swallowed up by huge conglomerates. Very rarely do they maintain the things which made the customers like them in the first place. So, does the modern BBC structure, in effect a takeover of the old BBC by a modern corporate ethos, really have a niche in it for the unique kind of serious speech radio which Radio 4 provides?

A more brutal question is how often, exactly, does senior BBC management remember that Radio 4 even exists, let alone falls in its area of responsibility? How many television executives recognize it as a medium demanding its own set of skills, and not just a larval or foetal form of television, or an apprenticeship for it?

Of course, some do. There are department heads of bi-media departments who really, really try, and all honour to them. But again and again we see evidence that the television service simply has no time to care about radio, especially Radio 4. When The Independent printed a long piece by Ben Bradshaw criticizing aspects of the BBC, two inches was about the problem of Radio 4 standards and management. There was a reply printed, from a very senior TV executive, a channel controller; he answered all the points, even those nothing to do with his own job; but how much did he say about Radio 4, in the reply to those inches of complaint? NOTHING. It's only radio. Whinging people in corduroy trousers.

When the BBC began, it WAS radio. That's all there was. By historical accident, British broadcasting has been distinguished by the fact that its founders were bowled over by an idealistic vision. They never had the chance to think of it as a money-spinner; under Reith there were grand cultural ambitions. It's fashionable to snigger at John Reith now, but under those beetling brows was a real intention: to broadcast into every home "all that is best in every department of human knowledge, endeavour and achievement". It meant dance bands and comedy as well as heavy talks. Reith's henchmen were often romantics; remember CA Lewis's excitement about the plays and concerts:

"The shepherd on the downs, the lonely crofter in the farthest Hebrides, the labourer in his squalid tenement, the lonely invalid on her monotonous couch, may all in spirit sit side by side with the patrons of the stalls for the best performances in the world." He saw the forest of suburban radio aerials as "spears against the sky", fighting the war against ignorance and misunderstanding.

The pioneers saw broadcasting – radio broadcasting – as a greater revolution than Caxton's printing press; early books were expensive things for the few, but a radio broadcast was for the many: cheap to make, cheap to hear, a cultural and national blessing. That's the ancestry we have here: that's how our radio was born. That is what you breathe, in the air of Broadcasting House; as John Humphrys once remarked, a building which makes certain demands on you.

In the process of that birth, and right up into my own memory, there was a curious BBC ethos. Reithianism began it, and it grew into a mixture of mad bureaucracy and breathtaking editorial independence for producers, of petty regulations over small things yet big things being taken for granted. It was, despite its size, an oddly collegiate body. Robert Robinson once said, in the '60s, the BBC does the right thing by tradition and instinct, and the wrong thing is just an aberration.

But history means we no longer have that BBC. Some of the core values are still there, but commercial pressure, satellite pressure, technological pressure, political pressure and the fight for the licence fee have made the television service feel itself almost wholly ratings-driven. It is an expensive medium, and its overwhelming and understandable need is to point to large audience figures and say, "Look, look, we got bums on seats, we're worth it". Never mind what's being fed to that audience, never mind if they're paying much attention; raw ratings are the creed of all modern television, just as wide profit margins are the creed of all big business. But to take that parallel again: when big business is put in charge of a more modest, craftsmanlike, thoughtful, traditional business, where people make things with love and pride because those things are worth it – what happens? There is a clash, and a squeeze, and complaints that the profits aren't high enough for the capital value of the plant. So usually the small company ends by being closed down. And then there's nobody left to pass on the craft.

You can't control speech radio ratings in simplistic television ways: buying big stars rarely helps. You're more like an old-fashioned publisher, a Gollancz or early Faber & Faber, working on faith and idealism. All you can do is to make, and pump out, and publicize (till lately that's been our Achilles' heel), the very best, most passionately made and crafted, programmes possible. In a sense, a service like Radio 4 always has to be made for its own sake: you have to believe that if even one person is swayed, or inspired, or changed, or comforted by a programme, then that programme has been worthwhile. The raw numbers game can't be the beginning and end of it. You can't make it by formula or focus group.

Why does all this matter? Sometimes the comparison is made by defenders of Radio 4 between fine quality crafted radio and things like opera or ballet or symphony orchestras, which may be elite but which are worth preserving for the sake of the culture at large. But I say tonight that radio is MORE worth preserving; because it's bloody well free to all, unlike opera. I know people with NO money, MINIMAL social status, basic education – left school at 14, the older ones – but who always have Radio 4 on and listen, as of right, to important contemporary scientists and historians and actors and artists talking about their knowledge and their craft. I know people who have never been to London, who work with their hands, yet can make as sophisticated a joke as any you'll hear in Notting Hill ... they're up to speed, they're in the swim. Radio 4 plugs them in to everything worth hearing. These people – and OK, there are not nearly as many of them as there are people who sit in front of the television or listen to pop all day – they will say to you that it's their university, and their friend.

There are flaws and dead wood in the network. But when those who know how to make good radio are allowed to get on with it, and not circumscribed and starved of funds and equipment, there flows from Radio 4 a steady stream of inventiveness, humour, and intelligence which has enriched national life and – because of its cheapness and freedom to experiment – fed the television service ideas.

It is still common to see some press fanfare about a TV documentary "scoop" on a scientific or artistic subject, and to remember hearing all about it on Radio 4 six months before. Derek Cooper was first with the news of BSE; From Our Own Correspondent warned us about the Indonesian meltdown weeks ahead of any other mass medium. But that kind of radio – especially Radio 4 – IS endangered. By several factors. The most superficial is that, as those signs in foreign hotels say, THE RADIO IS CONTROLLED FROM THE TELEVISION. Within the core of BBC power there are television-trained people who are impatient of Radio 4, and irritated by its pretensions, and bored by its lack of technical wizardry and hot pictures and press coverage and general sexiness. They have no fellow feeling or kindness for it. No TIME, in their busy busy lives, to listen to it. Of course, there are individual bi-media managers who do their best for radio; salute them.

But if you wanted to be really unkind, you could say that with the new power structure of bi-media departments, Cain has been given the key to his brother Abel's life-support machine.'

Cain and Abel! I reproduce it now, not because I still think that is the case but as a nugget of what you might call the history of attitudes and fears. My rant was reasonably well received, though one senior executive (you know who you are) decided to please his masters and challenge it by sneering that perhaps people "of my age" found change difficult. I may have given him an earful. He's only half a dozen years younger than me.

But there was truth in the sense that Radio 4, in particular, was starved of necessary respect, autonomy and resources:

that many had a sense of being managed from a foreign power (i.e. TV), and yearning like a modern Scot-Nat for devolution. Or even for the BBC itself even to retreat, tend its own garden and defend its old core, telling vindictive governments that it needed the licence fee not in order to be a top act in the global strip-show but to offer, to any who would listen, Reith's vision of "all that is best in every department of human knowledge, endeavour and achievement".

Well, it was a good try. And thank God, my fear has not been entirely justified by subsequent history. Partly because radio skills have emerged, brilliantly, in independent production companies like Whistledown which can now sell to the BBC (and are indeed being urged to produce fully 60 per cent of non-news output). There have been some strong Controllers, notably Helen Boaden and Mark Damazer. So it didn't turn out as disastrously as I feared. Radio 4 is still looked down on by some in TV, and promoted too ineptly. But it survives. And though that rant was not about this book's subject, the Midweek programme, because the art of talk is non-technical and can always be revived, I included it because it brings back a strong sense of that period.

A period which also, by the way, saw the birth – on Radio 4 – of Steve Coogan's immortal character Alan Partridge. Since the diversity of his guests on Knowing Me Knowing You was at times quite close to the profile of Midweek guests, I had for a while some pleasure in being able to end the programme with "and on that bombshell …" as a form of homage to the great Partridge. In his desperate link-speak and crass line of questioning, the character was and remains a most useful warning to all of us who attempt radio talk. Every few days you can catch a Partridgeism on air, and not only from beginners.

But it was a hard time for the broadcasters at the sharp end. John Birt as DG was, I suppose, fighting for the BBC's life under a pretty hostile government, and had his reasons. Some still think him a benefactor. But as our generalissimo, he massively demoralized the poor-bloody-infantry, especially in radio. At one point the producer and I were summoned to listen to a commissioning editor reporting on what focus groups had said about the nine o'clock programmes. "It'll only take twenty minutes." We rapidly found that it would only take twenty minutes provided we respectfully asked no questions and made no comments, so as the management figure read on, Ronni and I became increasingly restless. To sum it up, by and large Midweek came out a shade above Start the Week at the time, on the grounds that people felt less intimidated by the cerebral tone of the latter. So before the droning was quite over, Ronni, a magnificently blunt-spoken woman, broke in saying, "OK. So what you're saying is – if we do interesting stuff, they'll be interested in it, and they'll like that?" Summed it up, really, and for a lot less money than the consultants.

It was late in this Birtian period, in 1998, that the newly appointed Controller of Radio 4, James Boyle, decided to revamp the schedule. All Controllers like to move the furniture around a bit, and all Radio 4 ones get taken aback by the resulting fury of accustomed listeners. Watching this process is always entertaining. A few years later, I particularly relished the contumely that fell on poor Mark Damazer later on when he removed Fritz Spiegl's "UK Theme" from the dawn, with its sweet medley of Rule Britannia and Scottish, Irish and Welsh traditional airs. His big mistake was to say it got in the way of a "pacy news bulletin", and the very word "pacy" had him excoriated as if he was some sort of shock-jock. Though God knows, this cerebral, earnest, academic figure (later Master of St Peter's College, Oxford) was anything but. Later on, I used to barrack him about it, just for fun, since as a sailor I had liked waking up in harbour to a bracing "Early one morning" and Rule Britannia. Mark was the kind of Controller who often turned up at the end of the show to meet the guests, and there was one fine moment when the unspeakably glamorous and hip Frenchwoman, Arielle Dombasle (the philosopher Levy's muse and wife) was on, clad in tight novelty newsprint leggings and a cloud of alarming elegance. Damazer came down at the end of the programme to commune with her (why shouldn't Controllers share some of the celebrity fun?) and rashly tried to explain that I had been teasing him about the morning tune. In the course of his explanation Mark Damazer burst into song, doing a spirited Rule Britannia to the alarmed chanteuse. Sadly, the tape wasn't running.

Anyway, back in the '90s Controller Boyle hit one of these periods of "must change everything", and did some useful things (though he rather castrated Radio drama, with too many 45-minute miniatures.). To us he announced that Start the Week and Midweek would shrink to half an hour: twenty-eight minutes or so after a shorter news bulletin.

Why? we asked. "You have no idea", he said, sorrowfully, "how much pressure I am under." Birtianism and ratings-mania had got an iron grip on the poor man. There followed what I like to think of as the Grand Remonstrance (a phrase vaguely remembered from O level history – grievances presented to Charles I by Parliament in 1641). It marks the only time I have ever had a chance to fight a battle alongside Melvyn Bragg. He and I went up to the office to explain to the fretful Scotsman that in a live programme with four guests, dropping one was risky to its internal ecosystem, and if someone got stuck in rush-hour traffic (not uncommon) we would be down to two. Who might be the least worthwhile two. Melvyn was brilliant, reasoning calmly and kindly. I just ranted.

The outcome was that Melvyn and I both agreed to do dummy programmes at twenty-seven minutes, so the Controller could see how awkward a talk show of that duration might be. We used volunteer guests primed to return the following week for the real programmes. I am not saying that either Melvyn or I sabotaged the dummy shows. But we half won: both shows got fifteen minutes back. It was a limited victory, but in this trade a rare one, and we went to forty-three minutes. It did mean that due to the anally strict evening schedule shape, the evening repeats needed to come down to just under half an hour (this was long before you could get the full programme online on listen-again) So for all the years of this shortening, producers had to spend half the day editing out fifteen minutes for the evening slot: a task famed as one of the most unnecessary and useless deployments of producer-time on the network. On the other hand, it meant those producers got a chance, in the cold-hearted privacy of their screens, to assess how well the conversations went. That was probably educative. A silver lining.

From that day until its end, Midweek, like its Monday sister, ran from 09.02 or so until 09.44, with four guests and just one presenter. A rough familiar shape developed: you risked less time for round-table conversations (especially if a story is complex, or a guest slow-spoken) and needed a careful eye on the clock. Perhaps the first guest ended about 09.14, the second ran to 09.24, and so on. If there was music to illustrate a musician's work we couldn't afford more than a minute, and usually just one piece. A live playout was always fun, so the host could say a brisk goodbye before it started and then let Continuity fade it, while in the studio the rest of us sat happily enjoying the whole number.

It always delighted me when musicians were willing to play live: never less than when the sitar virtuoso Ravi Shankar was on. His "people" said severely that the Master absolutely could not play for the niggardly minute-or-so we could allow, because ragas are long, meditative and sacred. The effect of his promoters' sternness was to make us feel as if we were considered likely to breeze in with a chirpy "Oy, gissa tune, maestro!" But Shankar had his sitar on his lap while he talked, beautifully, about the instrument. And when I murmured, live on air, the possibility of him playing a bit, off he went: just for a neat minute, and happy to do it. Guests are often less trouble, and less precious, than their "people" give you to expect.

IT'S ALL ABOUT THE GUESTS

I really mean that. Midweek was never a vehicle for me to be a "radio personality", perish the thought. It is not the kind of programme that should ever have the presenter's name in the title, or attract a personal fan base, or involve some radio equivalent of the presenter coming down a big set of stairs like Parkinson, to tumultuous applause. When one stand-in ended, comedy-club style, with "I've been — —, you've been a great audience, thanks for listening", I flinched. I have been prissy enough always to end with the formula "among US next week will be …". Just to include the production team.

The presenter of Midweek existed only as a conduit for the personality, knowledge, experience and entertainment value of the guests. It is also my contention that the job was not to challenge them, Today-style, on every point (unless they're actually Nazi or libellous). The point was to encourage them to be the strongest possible flavour of themselves, so that listeners could make their own judgements.

One incident illustrates this: at the table was Sir John Junor, the much satirized "sage of Auchtermuchty" and editor of the Sunday Express for thirty-two years in its glory days. The question of feminism having arisen, he expressed his view that you wouldn't like to be in an aeroplane piloted by a woman because she might be having her "time of the month". I asked what he thought this mysterious "time of the month" felt like, and he expressed its presumed dreadfulness. Which, like many others with active wombs, I found quite funny. There were some furious letters later, asking why I did not shoot Sir John down. But my argument was, and remains (though it's unpopular in these days of hysterical online overreaction), that Midweek was more like a Natural History programme. Sir David Attenborough would not challenge a badger – "Why do you eat hedgehogs? They do you no harm! And what's that silly black and white striped snout about?" Rather he would say, "Shhhh ... quiet ... keep very still and the badger might come out further so we can have a good look at him." I wanted Junor to be as Junor as possible, that's all. Listeners are not stupid. They can decide who they like and who they don't. Some guests I have really disliked, but I defy you to name them. In the same way, if you are interviewing someone who claims to have been snatched by aliens, it is always more enlightening to ask "What did they look like? Did they give you anything to eat?" than to say "I don't believe you". Challenges are for news, for demanding answers from the powerful, or for debate programmes. I can do that too, and grew up doing it on Today. But it wasn't the point. The point was to catch the gamey, honest, fascinating human flavour.

So here are some memories of guests, good, bad, inspiring and incredible. They are selective, because memory is a selective faculty and mine is no better than average.

THE TRICKY GUESTS

Get these over with first, because they are remarkably rare. People often ask whether it is difficult to "control" people live on air, but actually it is far harder to pep them up than calm them down. Something about Radio 4, for good or ill, motivates people to behave decorously. Sometimes that is a pity. There is a certain refreshing quality about irritability, even when directed against one's hapless self. When I said to Denis Potter that he was being called an elder statesman of TV playwrights, he replied, "If you call me that I shall bite you on the leg."

One thing I have only encountered once is a drunk guest – I can't bring myself to name him, because he was a much-loved figure in his prime. But I can tell you that the romantic view of the "Renaissance drunk" with voluble, fabulous Dylan Thomas eloquence is well wide of the mark. What really happens when someone is drunk is that a sort of elephantine thoughtfulness kicks in. "Well – the answer to that is in two parts. No, three. But the first point is this, that there are two things, and two things that – well, four parts really. What I want to say is ..." Nightmare.

The only guests who really made things hard – apart from mere shyness, rapidly cured by the quiet, invisible intimacy of a radio studio – were those who were aloof. The ones who didn't want to listen to the other three, and who emanated a weird sort of chilly disapproval as if they had been forced by their PRs to do this pathetic show. They have been very rare, but my remembered shudders are about the union leader Clive Jenkins, who radiated disapproval of all the rest of us, and about Christina Foyle of the famous bookshop, who answered monosyllabically and with disdain, and did not appear to listen to any of the others. It was difficult too when a guest (invariably a male rock star) would not remove his sunglasses, which slightly alienated the rest of the room.

But occasionally you got someone who, without meaning to at all, utterly intimidated the rest of the group to the point that when he left the room afterwards an excited chatter broke out, exactly as if the headmaster had swept out of a particularly fraught assembly. The most striking of these was Enoch Powell. He didn't intend to create this vacuum of joviality but effortlessly did. Not least because of his response in the green room, when politely and shyly asked by the poor researcher (in fetching leopard print leggings) whether he would like the Gents before the show. It was two floors away, owing to the refurbishment. Enoch fixed her with those extraordinary hypnotic blue eyes and said in that high, otherworldly voice, "No ... I speak with more passion on a full bladder."

Not relaxing. But he was civil, and interesting, and if the rest of the room quailed a bit, I am sure Mr Powell didn't mean it to happen.

The precise opposite of a tricky guest was one who was such a source of warmth, strength and comfort that everybody else expanded and became more beautifully themselves. Premier of these was Dame Judi Dench. On the two occasions she was on, I might as well not have been there: I would ask the questions, whereupon everybody in turn would tell their story, or explain their skill or their pain or pride to Judi. And at the other end of some sort of spectrum, I would mention that one of the most relaxing, jovial presences in any studio is "Little" Jimmy Osmond. He's been on twice: frank and interesting about growing up as a Mormon and helping his family through tricky times, but also so visibly pleased to meet everyone else that before the show that he offers to hand round the tea and eagerly asks, "What are you gonna talk about? You've written a book? Awesome!" It is amazing how happy this makes people.

Rarest of all are the moments of actual hostility on air, and I suppose I should relate the most famous. Though at the time – in the ten minutes before the phones started going mad and newspapers chasing us – the producer and I honestly thought very little of it, merely wondering vaguely whether we should cut some swear words from the evening repeat.

This was the encounter between Joan Rivers and the black activist Darcus Howe. He had made a programme about tracing a son he didn't live with as a child but found as a young adult. Joan was increasingly restive about this "babyfather" history and gradually took against his campaigning stance. It proceeded thus:

Joan: "I'm so bored with race, I think we should all …"

Darcus: "You are entitled to be bored by it, I am not."

Joan: "Yes you are, yes you are, let me explain, I think people should intermarry, everyone should be part this, part that and part everything, and race doesn't mean a damn thing, it's about people … everybody just relax, take the best of their back cultures and move forward."

Me (emolliently, without effect): "That's a very American approach, a melting -pot approach …"

Darcus (loudly): "America is the one of the most savagely racial places …"

Me (inaudible)

Darcus: "So since 'black' offends Joan …"

Joan: "Wait – no – just stop right now! Black does not offend me – how dare you! How dare you say that! Black offends me? You know nothing about me – you sat down here and …! The USE of the term black offends me? – where the hell are you coming from, you have got such a chip on your shoulder, I don't give a damn if you are black, white, couldn't care less, it's what the person is – don't you dare call me a racist –I don't know you."

Darcus (attempts a laugh, half-audible)

Me (deciding to calm things down a bit): "I don't think it was personal, Joan."

Joan: "Oh, I think it was! When someone says the term black offends Joan! I will not sit there and have you say that."

Darcus: "I think this is a language problem."

Joan: "No, I don't. I think this is a problem in your stoopid head. You had a child, you left them, your wife said you weren't there, you married a woman, you deserted her, now your son comes back and he's got problems – Don't you dare call me a racist – don't you dare. I will not ..."

Darcus: "Can we continue?"

Me: "I have great sympathy with both sides." [Actually, I really did, Darcus was being patronizing and patriarchal, but Joan was overreacting. I thought so anyway.]

Joan: "Sympathy? Then YOU'RE a racist! (to Darcus) Don't you dare call me that! Son of a bitch!"

I did say at one point, "Darcus, can we just hear you saying that Joan is not a racist?" but that set him off again, saying "I don't know if Joan is a racist." So of course, she too set off in hot pursuit.

It quietened down, but Joan was so genuinely angry that – scheduled to do her interview next – she said she would rather be on at the end. So I looked at the fourth guest, an eminent botanical photographer, who was sitting there frozen in horror. And I said, "OK, let's turn to talking about plant photography."

I am happy to say that this sentence found its way, according to my cabaret and panto star friend Iestyn Edwards, into the backstage vocabulary of those trying to defuse rows between excitable performers – "OK, darling, let's talk about plant photography." A brief immortality.

Anyhow, Joan did her own interview in the end, Darcus stayed quiet, the phones went mad demanding comment, and I had to go on the PM programme and explain to Eddie Mair that no, I really didn't think it was my job to prevent this happening. These were grown people, both genuinely aggrieved, on a grown-up channel. I was not their nanny.

They had a right to say what they felt. That is the point of live broadcasting.

Midway through the afternoon Joan Rivers rang me at home in Suffolk and said,

"Hey, honey. Sorry. Did I call that guy an asshole, on the BBC??"

"No, Joan. Sonofabitch."

"Oh, thank Gaaaad!"

It ended up being our finest hour in publicity terms. I never minded it when things got beyond control for a while and I sounded like a fool trying to calm it down. As a listener myself, I know perfectly well that people actually enjoy thinking "Ha ha, get out of that, Purves!". It gives a moment's pleasure to those who don't like me, and a chance for sympathy for those who do. And – like the occasional phone going off – it proves the damn thing is live. Though frankly, if we'd had Jimmy Osmond at the table it would probably never have kicked off so viciously at all. He would have said "Awesome" and we'd all have felt thoroughly hygge again. Maybe.

SWEARING

We haven't had much. People tend to know they shouldn't do it on Radio 4 at nine in the morning. So whenever they do, it is memorable. Especially when unexpected: you can warn off all the comedians but then find that an elderly marine biologist, telling about an encounter with a Scottish fisherman, drops the man's instinctive f-word into a quote. Or, on another occasion, a dark-skinned guest remembered being called a "fucking nig-nog" by an immigration officer. After that we got a fine letter from a listener saying "thank you for permitting the intelligent use of that phrase".

The one really gratuitous f-word came from Jeremy Irons, years ago, when I was probably annoying him by talking about the very establishment-toff parts he had been playing since Brideshead Revisisted.

"Do you ever feel you want to break out and do something different?"

"Like saying fuck on the radio?" he replied, and instantly regretted it. The tabloids did a bit of "Toff Jeremy swears on radio!", but I made no comment and moved on. I always do. Officially we're supposed to "apologize to the audience on behalf of the guest", an instruction which I consider downright creepy. Once, a woman who had lived on the streets and gallantly hauled herself back to respectability was quoting the abuse she got, and used the f-word again. The producer Chris Paling said down the talkback that I should apologize at the end of the show.

I didn't. I wasn't going to embarrass the poor woman like that. For heaven's sake.

Afterwards Paling said mournfully,

"You didn't apologize when I told you to."

"I know. You knew I wouldn't."

"Yes, that's good, but it's my job to tell you to."

On which subject, by the way, it was the late Aubrey Singer, Managing Director Radio, who in the 1980s gave a definitive judgement. "If these words crop up in the heat of the moment, as on a picket line or in a live interview, fine," he said, "but I will not have people sitting down and typing them out."

It is a beautiful rule. Mind you, there was also a diktat at that time that you couldn't say "Bugger" in a southern accent, but it was all right to say "Booger" if you were Northern. No, I have no idea whether that still applies. Best not to ask.

But it is remarkable how little people actually do swear, and how rarely they get aggressive. Vinnie Jones was gentle as a lamb, and when I flailed for a moment over relating a famous moment when the footballer grabbed a fellow player by his – er – male – er – intimate bits, it was Vinnie who chipped in politely. He finished my sentence with "Threepenny bits". What a gent.

Unlike the American general who, talking about Vietnam, annoyed me first of all by his boast that he always made sure troops under him got "clean whores". I didn't challenge that, though I should have. But a moment later, when he was saying how hard the war was for his guys, I murmured that it was pretty hard for the Vietnamese too. He went silent, then after the programme turned to me in the green room, looming over a chestful of invisible medals, and said loudly, "You, ma'am, are a bitch!" Yep. In that context, proud to be.

MEETINGS OF MINDS

Much of the pleasure of the programme has been in encounters between guests who might not normally meet: odd bonds and empathies, a web of understanding forming across the table. The people you expect to take an interest in one another don't necessarily do so. Of course, producers think in advance that two will get on, or sympathize, but they are more concerned usually with a balance of tone, pace, voice and topic. And as often as not, it is an unexpected voice which brings up an enlightening and bonding parallel experience or feeling. A musician and an archaeologist, a surgeon and a cabaret artist, a dancer and a gang survivor, a 9/11 firefighter and an inventor of word games, a football referee and a vicar: any pair or trio may suddenly flare into mutual enthusiasm. Sometimes there is a lasting result: only one marriage so far, but several friendships and collaborations. At the beginning of the 1990s Richard Ingrams, who had left Private Eye, and the publishing entrepreneur Naim Attalah were on together. Richard claims grumpily that "Libby kept butting in" (it is hard for some chaps to notice the clock ticking), but that meeting with Naim at the table led, eventually, to the foundation of The Oldie magazine. Hurrah.

The shortening of the programme under James Boyle made that interaction harder to get in, but if you have economical speakers who give the essence of their story or craft quite briefly there is often good space for it. Agreeable moments come up: the drummer Ben Goddard, who had smashed several keyboards up with "a very heavy right hand" playing Jerry Lee Lewis during the run of Million Dollar Quartet, showed his prowess in the studio on a borrowed keyboard. Egged on by me saying "Go on, the BBC can afford it!" he bashed hell out of it, while next to him a Benedictine monk said approvingly, "That would really cheer up Vespers."

I gave the example of Bill Roache and Carlos Acosta, but at least both of them were in showbiz of some kind. There was a beautiful moment between two poets once, too: Seamus

Heaney listening, eyes closed, while the Jamaican Jean Binta Breeze read her poem. A less expected kinship arose between Kelvin Mackenzie, the tabloid bruiser from the Sun, and a woman who had lived rough as an alcoholic and recovered. He was in huge sympathy with her, both of them agreeing that they just wanted the nicest house and lifestyle they could get, and why not?

Their bonding was to some extent a mischievous ganging up on another guest, a Greenham Common protester and banner maker of immaculate socialist peacenik instincts. At one stage she challenged Mackenzie and media news values in general, explaining that on the day that a global women's mission went to Beijing there were dozens of supporters at Victoria Station. Yet this beautiful occasion, to her disgust, wasn't reported. She felt this was because the papers were full of "some film star arrested with a prostitute": Hugh Grant.

Kelvin Mackenzie turned to her and with heavy courtesy said, "Madam, I am sure you are a very intelligent person, but I have to tell you that you do not have a future in journalism."

Sometimes the crossover was unexpectedly, bruisingly moving. Monty Roberts, the "horse whisperer" had memories of a bad, possibly violent relationship with his father. He found himself sitting next to Lord Linley, who spoke with immense affection and gratitude about his father Lord Snowdon and the love, encouragement and artistic inspiration the photographer gave him in his own work as a designer. Monty Roberts was momentarily overcome by a kind of grief at the contrast with his own memories, close to tears, needing a pause. At other times the endurance, suffering and redemptive vision of one guest – a hostage, a war survivor, an innocent Death Row prisoner recently – has stilled the table. Nearly always the moment is deepest when it is at least a little redemptive, because raw suffering without hope is hard for anybody to digest.

But there is a healing quality about hearing of it sometimes: Dr Ann McPherson speaking with calm rationality in her own terminal illness about the right to die; or lately, a moving reflection on home and exile which arose from a conversation spanning China and wartime Europe. Arno Geiger, whose book "The Old King in His Exile" was relating his father's dementia and his confused demands to go home even when he was there. He connected this to the old man's long-buried, dark memories of horror in his teenage war service, far away in a Red Army hospital crammed in with the dead and dying. The old man used to say "Never leave home!" and after the war he never again did: but then his dementia made him fear he had. Xiaoulu Guo, speaking of old people living through China's change from a peasant economy to hard urban capitalism, talked then of an endemic sense of dislocation and loss of home; listening were the percussionist Evelyn Glennie and the comedian Milton Jones. Which may seem random, unconnected: yet in moments both heard and unheard, their presence warmed the room, gave flow to the conversation. These things feel like a web of understanding, a proper human moment. When the programme was at its best – and of course no programme always is – we discovered that listeners felt it too.

I have treasured the unexpected enlightenment that comes from the diversity of the guests. Chris Rapley, an ice-core scientist, shared the table with two musicians (one being the pop star Jamelia), and casually the question came up of what music he took with him on expeditions. He explained that he wouldn't take music he liked and which really meant something to him, because, spending weeks on end in a frozen wilderness, it would just make him homesick. So the expedition listened to noisy, energizing disco instead. It was good to learn that. Just as it was good when a survivor of the Pol Pot years in Cambodia compared lives with Colonel John Blashford-Snell and a monk turned dancer. Or when Sophie Thompson talked about her imaginary zoo animals with Jonathan Franklin, who kept owls at Eton as a boy, and both listened to Leon Bosch, the double bass virtuoso talking of revisiting the cell where he was tortured in apartheid South Africa.

The producers worked always to balance out the weight and tempo and complexity of guests – sometimes torpedoed by a late cancellation or a sudden red-hot chance of a booking. I always flinched a bit when the research notes included too many dense books and complex stories, needing telescoping in a careful linking script so as to convey a lot of information quickly and get to the bit they tell best. But the point is that Midweek, unlike the other nine o'clock programmes surviving it, never did have a theme. John Goudie, one of our last editors, says he cherishes the memory of hearing Jeremy Paxman plaintively asking "Libby, what's the theme?", as he found himself on the way to the studio flanked by Priscilla Presley, a Brazilian ballet star and the transgender writer and brilliant memoirist iO Tillett-Wright, named after one of the moons of Jupiter. Actually, later on Jeremy peevishly asked iO which gender he was at the moment, and when he was told, asked "How long will that last?" "Who knows?" replied iO, gaily.

Some moments are bathed now in my mind in golden legend, yet they really happened. The late Master of the Rolls, Lord Denning, who deployed a pleasingly antique judicial manner and a fine West Country accent, was on in the early days alongside a newly crowned Miss UK. I was chuntering on, asking her ordinary questions, when he suddenly took over with all the majesty of the Bench.

"How long does it take you to get dressed for your pageants?"

She was a sparky girl, and replied,

"Dunno, how long does it take to get into your judge kit?"

"Oh, a long time sometimes, if I am in my Gold Robes. There are tights, you see."

At this point it befits a presenter to sit very, very still and quiet and hope against hope that the pair of them will get onto comparing suspender-belt technique.

Sometimes meetings are serendipitously suitable. Ken Clarke, appearing to talk about his political memoirs, was obviously enough of a jazz fan to warm to Soweto Kinch. Poets and performers often love to meet. I am not sure how much enlightenment Alistair Campbell got from keeping company with yodelling Frank Ifield, or Thora Hird from Bruce Dickinson of Iron Maiden; but Ray Winstone and Ran Fiennes were nicely alpha-male together. And Boy George was a perfect guest at responding to the others: so perfect that I used to urge the BBC to give him the presenting job on weeks I was away, or to create a new show called Boy George's Culture Club.

He was on Midweek with Cher's daughter Chastity Bono, a sensible, downbeat, pleasant young woman who later transitioned to become Chaz. I was teasing her a bit about growing up with such a highly roomed diva as Cher, and how any little girl would have longed to pinch her lipsticks and try out her false eyelashes. Chastity had no such wishes, and firmly said so, but it took only a flicker of my eyebrow to get Boy George piling in with squeaks of comic envy.

Sometimes it is an encounter with an unsung professional which brings out a sensational revelation. I remember the late Jim Prior, former Home and Northern Ireland Secretary, being on with a dog trainer and confiding – sadly, after the show was over – how he taught his own dog tricks. A bitter loss to broadcast history, and a lesson to me always to watch the body language during the programme in case there's someone who wants to butt in. Better luck with the moment when Brian Blessed, the stentorian actor, found himself sitting next to an admirable and experienced male midwife. Blessed suddenly confided to a stunned world that half a century ago in Richmond Park he found a woman in labour under a tree and delivered the baby personally, licking its face clean and biting through the umbilical cord.

My answer to this I wish to record, because these are the only five ad-lib words I have ever been subsequently proud of. I just found myself saying, "Brian, am I believing this?" Polite yet doubtful: I commend the phrase to you next time you feel someone may be bullshitting but don't want to insult them in case they're not.

Sometimes a moment of curious enlightenment comes over the whole group, and even if nothing is said about it by the others, you sense it in the room and over the air. I remember Sir David Attenborough, and this exchange. It was not long after his wife's death. I had asked him whether wildlife made him happy:

"Yes, I think that's so ... it's not quite the right word, but for example, I remember sitting in a hide on northern Australia, on the edge of a billabong. The sun comes up and there are myriad flocks of egrets and ducks, and crocodiles on the side, and kangaroos coming down ... They're all busy about their business and there's an extraordinary feeling of contentment. You watching it, and you know you've got no part of it."

The question came up from somewhere unplanned. Somewhere not unrelated to my own loss of a son.

"Is there – consolation in that?"

"Yes," he said quietly, "That's the word. There is a sort of consolation. In moments of personal trouble, and trial, there is huge consolation in looking out and seeing that there is actually a robin, come to sit on your windowsill, as it has and always will ... yes, consolation is the word." The moment meant a lot; the geese flying over our marshes in Suffolk console me still.

Sometimes, of course, it is not one of the guests but the presenter who is momentarily torpedoed by a line, spoken in the particular ease and intimacy and atmosphere of willing communication that a live radio programme can provide. The time around our son Nicholas' suicide – which was prefigured by a few years of growing, un-expressible, inchoate anxiety – was a vulnerable period for me. A few weeks before it happened, Cormac McCarthy's novel "Blood Meridian" was quoted, with the line:

"When the lambs is lost in the mountain, he said. They is cry. Sometime come the mother, sometime the wolf."

I felt that wolf prowling round my son, and though I had no idea of the form the monster would take, the line stopped me dead for a moment.

After Nicholas died there was some anxiety expressed about how, coming back to work after that summer's break, I would deal with guests with parallel or allied stories to tell. Should they keep away from suicides, lost children, any children? I firmly, indeed arrogantly, put a stop to any such inhibition and told the producer Chris Paling – a good friend by then – that he must pull no punches and allow no consideration of that sort. The presenter's feelings are simply not the point: as a mad old proverb from my childhood goes, "Be not a baker if your head be made of butter!" I remembered an absurd moment from some years before, when I arrived on a Tuesday afternoon and mentioned to a former producer that my father had just died suddenly. I had carried on with the trip to London for work because that was the ethos in which Dad brought us all up, and also because I needed to go to some government office to get a copy of the prayer said at CMG holders' funerals (this was pre-Internet).

When I explained why I was late, the producer went suddenly pale at the news and ran from the room: why should she be so affected? But it turned out she was hastening to another phone to postpone a guest, Julian Litten. As author of "The English Way of Death", he was to talk about the social evolution of funeral customs. The irony here is that I would have been very interested that week.

So, after the more shocking death, I felt there should be no quarter asked or given about guests who might worry the presenter. Chris Paling took me at my word, and I found myself able to deal with the hardest of stories, indeed was often fortified by them and by the astonishing human ability to accept fate. But shock can come at you from left-field, from the blind spot, suddenly. The only time I had to choke back a rising flood of inappropriate personal emotion was when David Shepherd, the wildlife artist and conservationist, began talking with pride about his nine grandchildren, and the pleasure of watching enthusiasms and talents flowing on down the generations. And suddenly there was the awareness in me, not fully realized before, that one branch of our own small family would never flower now.

But hell, you carry on to the next topic. And if I never felt such choked hesitations, it would be wrong. One is not a Vulcan.

PIECES OF HISTORY

I had chest pains one morning. Turned out to be nothing much, in the event: a pulled muscle. But symptom enough for the editor to want me to go to A & E. At half past eight. Argument raged, and eventually, petulantly, I won and didn't go until 9.45 after the programme. The reason for this perhaps stupid resistance on my part was because the programme would have to be taken off, and one of the guests was not only elderly and had travelled quite a long way, but was due to tell his story of tunnelling out of Stalag Luft III in 1944. To have sent a war hero home un-interviewed because of a wimpy twinge would not do. Not something one could live down. And to be honest, I was a bit depressed anyway, so if it killed me, who cared?

The producer watched, haggard-faced, through the glass in case I keeled over, but apart from the odd wince, all was well. But if it hadn't been, it would have been worth it. Meeting bygone heroes does that to you.

Another memorable veteran was Geoffrey Wellum, DFC, author of "First Light", a modern classic about his time as a teenage fighter pilot in World War 2. To such memories one cannot but listen, marvelling and slightly ashamed at modern softness. He had made a life in business since, married and divorced, but said that he needed to write the book to show to himself that he had done something real in his life. But the abiding memory came when he said that he had felt, as that 19-year-old Spitfire pilot, that nothing in life would ever be as good, as exciting, again. I asked him whether anything had been. Quietly, he said no. It opened a perception of that whole group of wartime lives: thrown into perilous adventure in youth, left drifting emotionally with a sense of anticlimax. The room went silent.

I feel privileged to have worked on a programme like this over what have been the last decades for many of that active wartime generation, few of whom made it into the new century. It has been an honour to meet soldiers, sailors, D-Day veterans, the women who worked in the codebreakers' huts at Bletchley Park, and not least, two of the female RAF pilots who delivered fighter planes and bombers across the country through the war years. One dashing lady veteran remembered looping the loop for fun, illegally, and arriving covered white as a ghost when her powder compact exploded.

Some broadcasting veterans turned up too, notably Harman Grisewood: actor, scholar, pioneering announcer, a founder of the Third Programme and an irresistibly light-hearted spirit. Remembering 1929, he explained how he got involved.

"I had nothing to do, so I found the man who did the Children's Hour, wrote and said 'Can I have a job?' He said yes, if I would read Sir Walter Scott. I detested the novel but as you got three guineas for three quarters of an hour reading, I gave up my wretched employment in the city and read this boring book called 'Ivanhoe' on the Children's Hour ... poor little children!"

His take on Lord Reith, the first Director-General, was a delight. He said that the importance of announcers in those days – they ran programmes – didn't make him feel at all important. "Because Lord Reith made you feel very conscious that you weren't important! At all! That was one of his fortés. I was very sorry for him, but I wasn't impressed by him. I think I was one of the first generation not to be impressed by 'great men' and he was one, a very very tall man. Impressive voice, all that ... but people of my generation just weren't very impressed."

Best of all was his equally unimpressed memory of Reith's successor, Sir Frederick Ogilvie, who wanted to relay to Germany the famous 1924 recording of the 'cellist Beatrice Harrison playing to the nightingales in a Surrey garden. The idea was to soften Hitler's heart:

"Yes, it's amusing, but he took it very seriously indeed. Said the Germans are a sentimental race, and if they heard this nightingale they would be moved to tears, I thought this was rather rot … because I'd taken the trouble to go to Berlin to see what was going on. A fellow announcer went with me, and we told the director-general that it was pretty grim."

It was always good to watch round the table the faces of newer generations – my own and far younger – responding in that sociable, intimate setting to these nuggets of real history. We heard memories of the young Mandela from his secretary; heard Albie Sachs, the great anti-apartheid campaigner, talking of imprisonment and of losing an arm and an eye to a bombing but wanting only to forgive, move on, and celebrate his country. Clarence Jones remembered being a young black lawyer in 1960, reluctant at first to be drawn in to Martin Luther King's cause but drawn to his side by a sermon – he did the voice most convincingly. "I began to cry when he talked about my mother, using Langston Hughes' poem, 'Life Ain't Been No Crystal Stair'. I thought of my mother, a domestic worker." He signed up, went to Montgomery, became part of that history.

Fragments of history always enthral, whether political or frivolous. It might be Jimmy Jewel or John le Mesurier; Deborah, Duchess of Devonshire remembering Kennedy's funeral; the Queen's best friend, Margaret Rhodes; or the heart pioneer Christiaan Barnard (who I found strangely difficult to talk to). Among us on a sleepy Wednesday morning there might have been a former prime minister, a Rothschild, a Tennant, a child of the Kindertransport … all sharing memories, before becoming memories themselves. And doing it live, amid fellow guests from other worlds, sharing the moment.

ACTORS

Actors are interesting. But often fragile. I admire them almost unreservedly, not only when they are performing great works but because they take on less great ones with vigour. They put themselves out there, sometimes enduring criticisms which often belong more rightly to a duff script, and apart from anything else, have almost superhuman powers of memorizing. Many of them are deeply serious readers and contemplators of great literature, some are writers. Yet all may sometimes have to convince themselves, for the duration of a run, that a duff play is actually OK, that the cast and director can save it. Or that a duff director's vision won't entirely wreck a good play.

I also admire them because I know I can't do it: tried, at university, and proved myself to lack the talent of becoming, channelling, an entire new character and convincingly radiating its essence. I often wish more critics, and dismissive audience members, remained aware of how strange and marvellous this acting business is.

Actors obviously suffer from being dragged in to studios first thing in the morning after evening performances – and sometimes even the first-night after-party – with all the buzz of hope, sentimental camaraderie, insecurity and alcoholic excess which such nights entail. They generally rise to the occasion. Most are remarkably mellow, considering: poor John Hannah got accidentally delivered to the wrong door by his cab, and Ronni Davis the producer says she found him "sitting forlornly" by the wrong lifts. One, who I blush to name, was generally considered a thoroughly likeable babe even though he said in the greenroom to the rather brilliant researcher Ursula "You're blonde, so I'll speak very slowly". We women can be strangely forgiving.

Many of the more glamorous actors, male and female, turn up looking reassuringly rough. That is the glory of radio. Few of us are varnished, some are downright dishevelled.

Americans, on the other hand, never seem to look rough at all. And despite late taxis or last-minute bookings, they generally arrive beaming, helpful and intent on putting on a magnificent show of being thrilled to be on the BBC. They shame us.

The happiest actors seem to be either those who have either hit a streak of good work for most of their lives, or have found a second form of creativity over which they have proper control. It doesn't even have to be writing: there's Greg Wise's bricklaying and carpentry, Douglas Hodge's singing and composing, and more keen knitters and embroiderers than you can count. But all actors have, in my view, a right to be tricky. Who wouldn't be, in such a precarious profession? Especially those who read reviews: Greg Hicks is a marvellous RSC actor, who also created a memorable part in the Arcola's "Clarion" as a dementedly patriotic newspaper editor. But across the studio table, with his tense physique wiry and honed by capoeira wrestling, it was like sitting opposite a powerful and very tightly-wound steel spring. Especially as, at the time, I was also the Times' chief theatre critic. The reason I cite him is that such is the comradely nature of the round-table format that Mr Hicks unwound and was fascinating.

I suppose it is the moments of comradeship which shine out. Maureen Lipman, always a favourite, was on once with Tracy Edwards, who in 1989 skippered the first all-female crew in the Whitbread round the world yacht race. She was getting a new crew together, and Ronni remembers Maureen saying to her "Now be honest, Tracy, wouldn't you rather come shopping with me than do all this battling with the elements? We could go to a nice café and have a lovely cappuccino. Surely that's better?"

Of course some actors, over the decades, have turned up more than once. And it is in the nature of their trade that if the peg is a new production and a pretty lightweight one, they are naturally more comfortable if the presenter at least acknowledges their heavy-duty RSC, National Theatre, Oscar or Oliviers pedigree. It's only civil. Just because you're playing Mister Funny-tie Custardface on a dire new sitcom, it's no excuse for forgetting that you were a stunning Richard III. The first time Simon Russell Beale came on, it happened to be when he was playing the King in the Pythons' musical "Spamalot", followed round by a man clip-clopping coconut shells. He was funny about the show (especially his "tap break", which involved artfully standing with his feet out of sight while everyone else did the work). But to remind us all of his real eminence, I respectfully quoted a line he once gave about how acting is "three-dimensional literary criticism". I asked what that meant.

So he talked, gravely and intelligently, about drilling into the depth of text and subtext. And after a bit I got back to the point and asked, "So what's the, er, subtext of the King in 'Spamalot'?" Without missing a beat, soberly the great Russell Beale replied, "Ah, deep down he KNOWS he doesn't have a horse." This is a sentiment so profound that it has become a family saying ever since. Deep down, we all know that what we do is just a bit of a sham. A clopping of hollow coconut shells and trusting to luck.

To list actors individually would be cumbersome; they inevitably form a strong cadre of guests, all the way from Kenneth Williams ("No, I don't mind being cast as camp, being so VERY manly and macho myself") to Jill Bennett (said she wouldn't talk about Osborne, but did, spontaneously, on the show with Lindsay Anderson). Standout moments have been with Greg Wise, Emma Thompson, Dame Judi, Callow, Russell Beale, Rylance – dozens of them. A moment that lingers in the memory is a discussion between Sir Patrick Stewart and the opera singer Bryn Terfel, about how deeply they let themselves identify with the role they are playing. I had had this discussion before, once notably with Jane Horrocks about how violently the role of Lady Macbeth had shaken her. But the different approach of the opera singer was interesting:

Bryn: "For me personally, it's very dangerous territory. I cannot consider myself an actor, but I am more within the descriptive side of the music, it's all in there … look at any Mozart score, and any movement, it's within the speed, the colour, the tempo, the instrumentation, it's all there."

Stewart: "No, there's more! I saw Bryn in 'Das Rheingold', in 'Sweeney Todd', in 'The Marriage of Figaro' – there is such emotion about your performances! It cannot just be contained within the music! I know the music gives you much, that we don't get from what we do but … there is so much you put into it!"

Bryn (firmly): "Sometimes it's just that when you feel the voice is working … if the singing voice is there, on a given performance, some nights it isn't a hundred per cent …"(Pauses)

Me: "When you're being a complete bastard like Scarpia …"

Bryn: "Yes, yes!"

Me: "Do you throw yourself into it? Is it difficult, as a mellow man?

Bryn "I have mellowed in the role of Scarpia, it's exactly this. At first I threw myself more into the acting, and it was detrimental to my singing performance. Towards the end of the Te Deum for instance, which gloriously finishes the first act, I was out of petrol for the second act, which is one of the most dramatic sections for two persons on the stage …"

Later, an eminent stage and opera director was indignant about this claim, saying that Bryn put as much real acting into each role as any great actor he had ever dealt with.

Directors are good guests too, all the way from moderns like Nick Hytner and Greg Doran, back in time to the legendary Frith Banbury. He was a great West End figure from the 1930s and '40s who came on a few years before his death in 2008, and in the green room delighted my daughter (at the time a teenager considering a stage career) by looking at her carefully and saying, "Yes – you have a good mask", – a theatrical expression not often heard since Noël Coward.

Producers too: we've had Bill Kenwright on, and Michael Codron, and Thelma Holt. When I asked Thelma whether she would tell actors if a show wasn't working, she replied, shocked, "Oh no, darling, I'm in the LOVE business. I'd speak to the director." Cameron Mackintosh enthused like a child about his animatronic pig in "Betty Blue Eyes", and I loved that. One never cares if the actual production doesn't reach the heights; we're all entitled to our failures. It's how much its creators care and plan and think that sparkles in conversation.

I enjoy hearing about the nuts and bolts. And yes, I am to some extent stagestruck, with an ineradicable fondness also for cabaret and performance artists: let's have a hand for Captain

Frodo the contortionist, Ursula Martinez of vanishing-hanky fame, Mrs Barbara Nice, the crowd-surfing housewife, and Dominic Mattos, the serious-minded religious publisher and part-time Ethel Merman impersonator (I seem to remember he got on very well with a Jain monk). Oh, and Iestyn Edwards, whose tales of playing a temperamental ballerina, dancing in a tutu in Iraq to entertain the troops, fitted in oddly well with a Masai bride and a discussion about the lost yachtsman, Donald Crowhurst.

Then, just so I can quote another fragment of recording we saved, there was Cassandro, the Lucha-Libre wrestling champion from Mexico. He was a delight, a man fighting Latino machismo with style in rhinestones and glitter and humour and heart-shaped nipple pasties.

"We're not loved in society if we're gay", he said. "I went through a lot of discrimination, rejection. So when I got into the wrestling business men I think got threatened by me, but I had had something, like a gift. Back in 1990 I started wearing the bathing suits, the pantihose, the hairpieces, the glitter, the long dresses."

To finish, he, Cassandro, provided an opportunity for the most rewarding kind of question, the one when you know the answer will be short and fit the end of the show nicely.

"I've seen online", says Purves learnedly, "how you once came on in a pink frilled dress, and a tiny little midget, a dwarf, somersaults out from under your skirt. And zaps your opponent. Do you do this often?"

"Yes, of course!"

God bless all entertainers. Though there are limits. There was a grumpy period in the early '90s when I put one rare interdict on the producer (not that they ever listen). I asked for NO MORE NOËL COWARD STORIES. We had been going through a period of aged thespians who remembered The Master all too well. The trouble was that the stories were hardly ever in any way illuminating. A typical one would be:

"So I was playing the piano, in the pit, and Noël shouted down, 'Who's playing the piano?' and I said, 'It's me, Noël – Johnny!' And Noël said, 'Well, you're playing it very badly'. He was marvellous, Noël, Marvellous."

Still, years later, Sir John Standing, who was doing his great turn of Coward songs at the Pizza on the Park, gave me the most memorable, beautifully Brylcreemed image of Noël, from his childhood. "A shiny man, everything shiny, his shoes, his hair."

BEFORE THEY WERE FAMOUS. OR INFAMOUS.

As stars rise in the celebrity firmament, a common expression on the show is borrowed from Private Eye's running joke: "Yeah, had him/her in the back of the cab one time." Tracey Emin was on before she was a Britart star; Mark Rylance when he first took over the Globe; Clarke Peters long before The Wire, Gordon Ramsay before was famous for getting so cross. There was a bright young violinist (with normal hair) called Nigel Kennedy. A young American called Bill Bryson, lately released from servitude on broadsheet newspapers, talked modestly about his travels through America in "The Lost Continent". Oh, and there was Helen Fielding, who – though we all loved her newspaper column about Bridget Jones – had not yet made a book or a stardom out of the hapless singleton. She just came on to talk about a rather earnest novel about aid workers. All spent their hour in the back of the Midweek cab. Watching their future lives has been fun.

Less fun to recall are those who passed through the studio during a time of hope and reform, and later relapsed or declined. I felt maternal, anxious but pleased, when Paul Gascoigne – Gazza – showed us his rehab diary and talked about his new stability. I shivered when the next collapse hit the news. Rolf Harris has, of course, been on (he's been on every programme there ever was, it seems to me) but I have no particular memory, certainly not of any misbehaviour. Perhaps the women around Radio 4 studios don't look like soft targets.

We never did have Gary Glitter, I don't think, but (now here's a nugget of history to forget) for a glorious couple of weeks in the '90s the glam-rocker presented Start the Week. Honest. He did. All I remember is that he got muddled near the end, lost the list of guests' names, and concluded with a squeak, "So thank you – er – thank you everybody!"

Worst in the annals of our own infamy is the only guest we absolutely know to have fooled us. As he fooled publishers and media around the world. It is a scar on any career to have listened respectfully to Binjamin Wilkomriski; but his book "Fragments" – a supposed account of a small child in the concentration camps of the Holocaust – was electrifying when we thought it was all true. When he was unmasked, in 1998, by a Swiss journalist, Daniel Ganzfried, there was universal shock, though it seems possible that he may have, after a difficult orphanage childhood, come to associate himself and genuinely believe he was part of that history. The book was withdrawn.

At this point it is worth mentioning that one of the most fascinating things about hardship stories is that the authors of misery-memoirs (like Dave Pelzer) are both more articulate about it and oddly less moving than those who are there to talk about their lives and achievements since, and skate openly but briskly over horrific experiences in childhood. Perhaps the more you write about unhappiness, the more you market it, the less real it seems. Maybe that is a psychological help. Those who prefer not to dwell on past misery but just acknowledge it are by far the more affecting. Redemptiveness is a powerful idea. Some of the most impressive people I have met over that table have been ex-convicts with really horrible childhood back-stories.

One I think of often, though I was told he later had another relapse, was a young star of Pimlico Opera's memorable prison production of "West Side Story". Freed, he came on to talk about the experience alongside a fine prison officer who had collaborated with the inmates' production in his own time. The ex-con told how the song-and-dance life had got him quitting drugs, cold turkey, so he could join the cast. I sentimentally hope he came good in the end, buoyed by that memory of a remarkable show and his Radio 4 moment. Because for all his history, he shone.

ARTISTS

You might think that talking about the visual arts and fashion design on the radio was pointless. Not so (Neil MacGregor on his own programmes proved that week after week, sending me scuttling to websites to look at Dürer engravings or Phoenician idols). In fact, some of the most engaging, unselfconscious and impassioned talkers are in those areas. We had the blind painter Sargy Mann, talking about how he worked with measuring sticks and, with vivid memory and delight, "saw" the colours go onto the canvas at the moment he applied them. We met Chinwe Chukwuogo-Roy, the Nigerian artist who did a portrait of the Queen for the Commonwealth Institute, and recalled how their conversation was enriched by a shared sadness, as both had lately lost their only sisters: it always seems to me that this humanity shows in the portrait, a view of the Queen we rarely see caught. We have had Andrew Logan, founder of the Alternative Miss World, who airily invited me to be a judge that year; Sister Wendy with her hypnotically, eccentrically intense understanding of religious art. Among the designers, we rejoiced in Stephen Jones and Piers Atkinson, milliners of two generations, in Wayne Hemingway, in Zandra Rhodes, in Thomas Heatherwick passionately defending the controversial Garden Bridge project. And among the fashion crowd, some twenty years ago, there was Bruce Oldfield.

Actually, Bruce and I made a jokey deal that when I turned 50 I would cast aside my humdrum slacks and jumpers and go to him saying, "Darling, make me over. Make me glamorous." Never got round to it, even over the seventeen years since that fateful date. Ah well.

SPORTSMEN

Sport and athletic stars are often better talkers than you'd guess from their breathless, often rather technical post-match interviews. As I am not a great follower of any sport, even sailing (I prefer to cruise vaguely around than race), I have to put the homework in if I am to ask questions to which their real fans would like the answers.

It has been educationally rewarding. I thought cricket bored me to distraction, but rather took to Ian Botham, and could have talked to Garry Sobers for hours once I had grasped how important he was. Motor racing leaves me cold, but to have talked with Jackie Stewart and understood the work he did for track safety is an honour. Again, it helped that the champions were in company at a simple table with people from outside their intense, rarefied world of sport. It made them readier to reveal the human impulses, longings and idlenesses we all share. It also showed up how strong is the parallel with the world of professional musicians. I lose count of the times when 'cellists or pianists found themselves in passionate empathy with athletes and sportsmen.

Other athletes stand out: Will Carling, when he was setting up as a motivational speaker (always a slightly ludicrous career change, but popular with weary business executives who like to think that what they do is not unlike being star athletes). Or Roger Black, who was so stunningly good-looking I became deplorably girlish. In my defence, he was on with Greg Wise, also indefensibly gorgeous in those days; the moment middle age hit me was when I realized I was looking at these beautiful young men with wholly maternal eyes.

But I suppose the most memorable of physical geniuses was the French high-wire artist Philippe Petit, who walked an illegally rigged wire to and fro between the Twin Towers in 1974. I had had to read his book sitting on the floor, so great was the vicarious vertigo. In the studio I held tightly onto the table as he happily described how it is to be 110 storeys high over New York, trusting only to your feet and your pole, turning and kneeling and bowing. But there was a sad beauty, and a sigh around the table when he said – this a year or so after the destruction – that he mourned for the loss not only of so many people but of those two towers. "They are mine. I have married them."

ON THE ROAD

We were fresh into the new century when two things coincided: our Radio 4 department unaccountably had some spare money, and the Corporation's anxiety reached one of its intermittent peaks about the lack of "regionality". The focus was on resisting the pull of London-centric culture (it was before Media City Salford opened). So, Midweek was sent out on the road in the autumn of 2002 to broadcast live. Not from big venues like the Edinburgh Festival or Hay-on-Wye (which crop up quite often for all the talk shows, and in any case are often virtual Hampsteads themselves) but from people's front rooms: people of no particular fame, with a line fixed up by the Outside Broadcast Unit.

This was catnip to me. I grew up on local radio tearing around in the Radio Car to random venues to see what happened, and after that had presented Today live from EU summits (dull), Beijing (unique) and HMS Invincible (eventful: a Sea Harrier crashed while we were watching).

However, a third factor in the Midweek tour was that I had a totally paralyzed left arm after a tricky dislocation, and the nerves took four months to regrow to a usable state. So I was typing a first novel with one hand and travelling up and down the country on trains, carrying a bag with some difficulty, to meet the team at each place. It may be that tempers occasionally grew short. We got lost quite a bit (producer at the wheel, teeth gritted). I remember her getting a bit snappish and berating me for apparent lack of enthusiasm one week – I may have been a touch too satirical about a dodgy booking. So the following week, I resolved to be upbeat and optimistic. She, however, had reached breaking point, so my hopeful chirrup of "Ah, Preston – a famous steel town of course!" was met with a sudden dramatic discarding of her BBC correctness. There was a yell from the wheel of:

"I don't care what kind of f—ing town it f—-ing is, I am never ever going anywhere near the f—-ing miserable North again."

That's what an overdose of regionality can do to a hard-working, highly-strung creative programme-maker. However, we had a good show there and one of our best ever in Newcastle, with a veteran foster-mother and a woman private detective who explained that nothing would ever have lured her down to poncey old London. One snag was that the BBC team, forever under the cosh to be both politically correct and regionally sensitive, got a bit pale when they discovered something which I – living in Suffolk – could easily have told them. There is a phenomenon not unrelated to the Brexit fiasco, now I come to think of it, that the further you get from London the less PC the jokes and attitudes. A guy in Newcastle innocently made a rape reference (no worse than the very funny Pam Ayres poem about the two ugly sisters from Fordham). And in Cumbria a dear old shepherd, greeting a very cool black Liverpool pop group, said with approving simplicity, "Eh, you lads have learnt our language well!"

The memories drift back: a crowded front room in Great Yarmouth where a dentist explained to me that he loved his job because "you're working on people's smiles!" A farm where they crossbred dogs with wild wolves for film work. A castle. A house waiting to be washed into the North Sea on a Lincolnshire cliff. I also remember that we had a particularly insinuating young woman researcher tasked with finding houses to broadcast from. She miraculously morphed into different personalities depending where we were. Whenever the team arrived we would find that she had become virtually a daughter of the house: working-class and down-to-earth in the Yarmouth B&B, Yah-yah Sloaney in the castle, dog-mad among the wolf breeders. It's a gift. Disconcerting, but useful.

Gradually movement in my arm – then wrist, then hand – returned, and peacefully we all limped back to the London studios that winter with a fully functioning set of limbs. But those were not the only live outside broadcasts we did. Once – in the days of Vic Lewis-Smith – we actually went to New

York. My children were so small that I would only go out for twenty-four hours, so memories of the city are confined to a jetlagged sense that every phone box might contain a half-dressed Superman, and a swinging deli sign saying SEND A SALAMI TO YOUR BOY IN THE ARMY.

But I do remember the programme, not least because we had on both Helene Hanff (of 84 Charing Cross Road) and Quentin Crisp. And in the hospitality area a third guest steamed effusively up to them holding out a hand and saying, "I loved your book, Miss Hanff!" Unfortunately, the blue-rinsed and puffily coiffed person whose hand she was grasping was Quentin Crisp. But it was on that show that, for the first time on the UK airwaves, Crisp delivered his deathless message which I have cherished and followed ever since: "Don't bother keeping up with the Joneses. Drag them down to your level, it's cheaper."

I keep that mantra in my heart alongside Simon Russell Beale's great truth recorded a few pages back: deep down, we all know we don't have a horse, it's only coconuts. It chimes with Orwell's insight that viewed from within every life is a succession of small defeats.

A more prosaic outside broadcast enterprise came when, two Christmases running in the early '90s, we did the programme from the farm kitchen in Suffolk, where at the time Paul and I were running a quixotic, marginally viable horse-drawn small organic farm. It was a fine traditional kitchen table, and the atmosphere pleasant: we still had our full hour then, and Paul was a guest interviewer (no travel expenses, see?). He did Robert Carrier, the great cookery writer, who cooked us some classy scrambled eggs; and Zoe Neill, daughter and successor of A.S. Neill at the Summerhill Free School. The cat expert Roger Tabor came too, and when our vast cat Guinness landed on his knee with a thump in mid-show, he said in astonishment, "Look at the SIZE of him!"

But the most memorable encounter in that kitchen was between Germaine Greer and Bruce Smith, chief groom and manager of the Hollesley Bay Prison Suffolk Punch stud which did great work with young offenders. I was able to tell him that some ten years earlier, Midweek had interviewed a Lambrianou brother, associate of the Kray brothers, about his life, jail and reformation: a key memory from his Borstal years was how much he had loved working with the horses at Hollesley Bay.

Anyway, the programme went fine. Bruce didn't really take to Germaine Greer, since in the chat before the programme she had told off our producer Ronni for not being really emancipated because she'd never tasted her own menstrual blood: "If it makes you sick, you've a long way to go, baby." Germaine headed back off to her smallholding pretty promptly, and Bruce stayed on after the programme to talk horses with Paul. As he finally left, he glanced at a twig broomstick propped outside the back door. "Her, she left her transport, then?"

Ronni also fondly remembers two other trips out on the road. One was in 1996, on the replica of Captain Cook's ship Endeavour in the Pool of London, after her voyage from Australia. Glen Campbell was a star guest. He agreed to play for us as long as he could have a particular type of guitar. We borrowed one from a music shop in Denmark Street, where they stipulated that the shop should be credited on air. Which of course didn't happen, but we didn't think in a million years that they would listen to Radio 4. So when the researcher returned it, she got it in the neck because they had indeed listened and were very miffed indeed. Campbell was professionally impressive: asked how long we wanted him to play, I think we said ninety seconds, and he played to the second. When he arrived on board with his nice city shoes and his lacquered hair (or was it a rug?), he was slightly bemused at finding himself on a sailing ship in the middle of the Thames. However, when he heard that the Queen was expected later that day he was in heaven. I overheard him amusing the young crew with dirty jokes, e.g. "we were so poor we had to beat the dog off to feed the cat!"

In Ronni's years, we also went to a croft near Inverness to taste whisky, which was agreeable, and met a female scallop diver; and to Cardiff Bay to record a New Year programme. We always had to record one for the post-Christmas doldrum, because nobody will willingly come to Broadcasting House. In Wales, she remembers:

"We couldn't find a celeb – I kept saying 'anyone but Max Boyce' and who did we end up with? – Max Boyce of course. Who actually was great fun, and got on well with the poet Patrick Jones and a former drug addict."

During that time, I was serving ten years as a trustee of the National Maritime Museum at Greenwich. And HRH The Duke of Edinburgh was marking fifty years of association with the Museum, as co-founder, trustee and patron. So, we invited him on for a special programme, an outside broadcast live from the museum. The idea was to mark his anniversary and the opening of the Neptune Hall.

HRH rolled up in his transport of choice, a black London taxi he drove himself. I'd enjoyed being on the board with the Duke and knew a little of his ways and tastes, so when it was suggested by the BBC that we should invite alongside him some eminent people of his generation, random admirals or whoever, I said, "No, he likes the young." So – alongside the Museum director Richard Ormond – we booked a Sea Harrier jet pilot who had landed safely after his cockpit dome exploded, and a young woman merchant officer who was shot and injured defending her crew from bandits who boarded it in harbour.

The Duke loved it. Talked about life after the unexpected accession of the Queen ("one just gets on with it") and the Navy, and his love of the museum. Wrote me a note afterwards saying that it was more fun than being interviewed "all on one's own". Who knew? All those years talking to the likes of Gyles Brandreth about playing fields or world wildlife, and he's been pining for the chat show circuit?

But the best moment was after the show. He had asked the injured woman officer, "Where did the bullet hit you?" "In the breast, sir!" She indicated the oblique glancing shot which had got her. Afterwards Prince Philip laughed and said to me, "So you'll tell me that women are good for the front line? I'm telling you," (he indicated a hand whizzing past his flat chest) "if she'd been a bloke – would've gone right past her!". For all the joke, though, his respect for the young woman officer was palpable. Especially when I asked "Could you have got away?" and she replied, shocked, that she had her watch to defend. He liked that.

So, while the abiding background memory is of various studios – lined with sound-absorbent Ryvita-like panelling, its foam microphone shields often adorned with silly faces (to the irritation of the engineers) – there were enough outside broadcasts to remind me of old days in local radio and in news. And occasionally the studio itself saw unusual things. A baby crocodile. Panned gold ingots and a natural crystal diamond from an Australian stream. Many documents and diaries one dared hardly touch. Elvis Presley's very own wallet. Meat Loaf's credit card (name, Meat Loaf). Several Olympic medals, which everyone always wants to handle.

And, on one happy occasion, the table saw a boxful of giant Malagasy hissing cockroaches. They hissed beautifully for the microphone. But there was a bonus: some weeks later a visiting BBC executive grandee from – I think – Manchester was in the hotel where we always put guests, just over the road. He fled in alarm when a huge cockroach ambled out of his bathroom: they really are spectacular, up to three inches long, heavily armoured with waving probosces.

The manager related his interlude of terror to senior colleagues and we got to hear about it. But it seemed unwise to mention that, er, we knew perfectly well which programme had brought that fearful creature and its less-than-wholly vigilant handler to the environs of Broadcasting House. Nor did we ever let on that many years ago, another guest – lately freed from a frightening Middle Eastern prison – had begged to smoke because in order to relate and relive his ordeal he needed calm. The other guests were fine with that, so we put a bit of tape over the smoke detector and he had half a cigarette during the show. Our first duty, as ever, is to the vulnerable guest. We are hosts, after all.

I hasten to say that this dodge wouldn't work now. Indeed, it took a couple of years of pleading before we got the artist Maggie Hambling to come on the show, because she didn't want to be smokeless. When she eventually did come, after giving up smoking for a while, it was to talk about her grand shell sculpture on the beach near Aldeburgh. I love the shell, but casually pointed out that the opposition from many in the town might be reasonable because while it is beautiful close up and from shoreward and seaward, its worst aspect – a rusty

L-shape – is the angle visible from Aldeburgh. Aldeburgh is a not-unfussy borough. Maggi was not pleased.

"Oh. So now we're an art critic, Libby, are we?"

That was in a curious period, when we were exiled to Bush House on the Strand while Broadcasting House refurbishment was under way. Another memorable interview in that studio was with Sheridan Smith explaining how she got the chihuahua to leap into her handbag seven times a week without fail in "Legally Blonde: The Musical". "I hide pieces of meat all around my person", she said gaily. "You should smell me after the show."

ENVOI

It has been a privilege. Not always easy. Every weekend I have dreaded the advance work on the notes: going through the research, scanning books and films, looking beyond them and trying to pinpoint what – in seven to nine minutes – will be best to talk about. I create a script of questions. Most of these are inevitably largely ignored on the day. But they have to be there.

Working out the running order is a problem which the producer and I have had to mull over. If someone is really nervous they will, ironically, be often happiest going first. The most likely joiners-in can nicely suit the last slot, because they will have been an audible presence beforehand. A shortish, quirky topic often works well as a starter, as everyone will have a view on whether they too want to go into space, fly a microlight four thousand miles in winter, or hand-rear wolf cubs. Following a very harrowing story with a light one needs to be thought about: but oddly, the visible and audible fellow-feeling of others at the table makes that all right. Indeed, it is easier than it used to be when I was on Today, linking tapes about appalling sufferings to the next item with nothing but a time-check as a bolster. On Midweek, even without the time-check, the problem was generally diffused by very fact that the other listeners in the room, however light their stories, had sat intently hearing the story of suffering.

Sometimes the twenty minutes or so in the "green room" were useful (it's not a green room now, it's an open alcove near the Woman's Hour empire). It gives you an indication of who might be shy, who is grumpy, who is eloquent and who is monosyllabic. It is rarely what you would expect. The most nervous guest ever was Lord Snowdon, and some of the most confident are people who have never been interviewed before. Again, the fact of being live – knowing they can't start a sentence again to get it perfect – often makes newcomers to radio more eloquent, not less.

But in that green room the feeling warms: already they have become real people, not research-notes. The most abominable lie ever printed about me was in a weekend magazine after an interview I reluctantly gave because the writer was the husband of a colleague and she begged me to. The slapdash young interviewer's unnamed "source" claimed that I never spoke to guests beforehand, but sat silently doing the crossword.

At the time, I didn't even do crosswords, and had always put immense importance on connecting with the guests first. Not to talk about their interview subject – you keep off it for the simple reason that polite people don't tell the same story to the same person twice within half an hour. But we chat about something. Anything. To do the crossword silently in a corner would be appalling. It's not the big actionable lies you mind, in a way: it's small ones like that. I suppose that this is another reason I like working live. If you do mistakenly pick up a wrong press cutting, your guests can contradict you and everyone can hear.

The oddest, darkest green room moment was on September 12th, 2001. We had just begun a new series and the producer Chris Paling and I were hanging out on Tuesday afternoon in what was then our office, the best one ever: a tiny room next to the balcony at the very prow of Broadcasting House, right under the ladder to the antenna.

The news broke of the attack in early afternoon. At first it sounded as if a light aircraft had crashed into a tower, an awful accident but containable within one's understanding. But as the immensity of it became clear, we gathered round television screens in other offices. Mad figures were thrown around on excitable London local radio networks: "Hundreds of thousands dead" etc. Before long we realized that as an unconnected, non-news talk show we would be taken off the air: on Wednesday the Today programme would have to carry on, surely, all morning. We prepared to hit the phones and stand down our guests. One – a US military veteran – had already rung in to cancel, and was trying to make his way home.

But towards five o'clock the word came from Helen Boaden, who was then Controller of Radio 4. Presumably after discussions with News (God knows what those were like, newspeople don't cede territory easily), she ruled that by nine the next morning listeners would damn well deserve a break. So, Midweek must go ahead.

We considered the guests booked, and they all seemed to us mature, grown up, unlikely to be crass or violently political. It felt necessary to acknowledge America's shock and suffering in the opening moments, so we did. All four had travelled or had friends in America. All said something brief before we went on. The most memorable was Dave Gorman, the comedian, who was there to talk about his beautifully frivolous "Googlewhack" expeditions. He had been in the US recently, as had most of the others. But what he said was universal: though both were thousands of miles away from New York, he admitted that his first instinct was "ring my mum". Yes. That was it.

The general view of commentators and the network after that day was that keeping the programme on air worked OK. It was sort of needed. What decision would be made today in such an event, I can't know.

It has been a good run, for half a life. I am grateful for the experience, the myriad meetings, the people both sides of the glass panel, and the half-dozen Controllers who let Midweek continue on its erratic, organic way. Only a very few guests have been dislikeable or dull. Most, through a rainbow diversity of attitudes and experiences, have shown me what grace there can be in humanity and how listening to one another in company is a hopeful and healing thing.